SING WE NOW OF CHRISTMAS

Study by C. Franklin Granger
Commentary by Judson Edwards

Free downloadable Teaching Guide for this study available at
NextSunday.com/teachingguides

NextSunday Resources
6316 Peake Road
Macon, Georgia 31210-3960
1-800-747-3016
©2015 by NextSunday Resources

TABLE OF CONTENTS

Sing We Now of Christmas

HOW TO USE THIS STUDY

NextSunday Resources Adult Bible Studies are designed to help adults study Scripture seriously within the context of the larger Christian tradition and, through that process, find their faith renewed, challenged, and strengthened. We study the Scriptures because we believe they affect our current lives in important ways. Each study contains the following three components:

Study Guide

Each study guide lesson is arranged in four movements:

Reflecting recalls a contemporary story, anecdote, example, or illustration to help us anticipate the session's relevance in our lives.

Studying is centered on giving the biblical material in-depth attention while often surrounding it with helpful insights from theology, ethics, church history, and other areas.

Understanding helps us find relevant connections between our lives and the biblical message.

What About Me? provides brief statements that help unite life issues with the meaning of the biblical text.

Commentary

Each study guide lesson is accompanied by an additional, in-depth commentary on the biblical material. Written by a different author than the study guide, each commentary gives the opportunity for learners to approach the Scripture text from a separate but complementary viewpoint.

Teaching Guide

In addition to the provided study guide and commentary, *NextSunday Resources* also provides a *free* downloadable teaching guide, available at NextSunday.com. Each teaching guide gives the teacher tools for focusing on the content of each study guide lesson through additional commentary and Bible background information. Through teacher helps and teaching options, each teaching guide also provides substance for variety and choice in the preparation of each lesson.

NextSunday
Resources

STUDY INTRODUCTION

A carol is simply a festive song, often of a dance-like or popular nature. Carol-singing was one of the pagan customs the medieval church adopted, initially at both Easter and Christmas.

The earliest English Christmas carol was written around 1350. The period from 1400–1550 was the heyday of the English Christmas carol. However, after the Reformation, some in the church suppressed the custom. Puritans saw it as a pagan activity, and John Calvin promoted singing only metrical psalms in the sanctuary. By contrast, Luther adored congregational singing and wrote several Christmas hymns in the style of folk songs and other popular tunes.

Throughout most of the 1700s the only officially permitted Christmas hymn in the Church of England was "While Shepherds Watched." The second carol to be approved, toward the end of the century, was "Hark! the Herald Angels Sing." Carols seemed to have had more success in remote country churches. Over time, carol-singing left the church and became focused in the home, the streets, and the meetings of religious dissenters.

Carols were finally brought into the mainstream of Anglican worship in the mid- to late nineteenth century. J. M. Neale published Carols for Christmas-tide in 1853. The cathedral choir in Truro, England, switched in 1878 from singing around town on Christmas to having an evening service inside the church consisting of two Scripture lessons, prayers, and a sermon, interspersed with carols. Two years later, the service was expanded to nine lessons and carols, providing the model used in 1918 at King's College, Cambridge.

In this unit, we will explore some of the familiar prophecies, as well as the Gospel birth narratives, through the lens of five traditional Christmas carols. As carols have grown to be a fuller and more meaningful part of our worship and celebration, so too can the stories of Jesus' birth continue to grow within us and enrich our faith experience.

The Penguin Book of Carols, ed. Ian Bradley (London: Penguin, 1999).

Until the
Son of God Appears

Jeremiah 33:14-16

Central Question

How will I prepare for the coming of the promised Christ child?

Scripture

Jeremiah 33:14-16 14 The days are surely coming, says the LORD, when I will fulfill the promise I made to the house of Israel and the house of Judah. 15 In those days and at that time I will cause a righteous Branch to spring up for David; and he shall execute justice and righteousness in the land. 16 In those days Judah will be saved and Jerusalem will live in safety. And this is the name by which it will be called: "The LORD is our righteousness."

Reflecting

As we sing in worship during the Advent and Christmas seasons, we don't often think about the stories and backgrounds of the traditional hymns and carols that fill our hearts and voices. Some of these beloved, familiar songs were centuries in the making. For the next five weeks, we will let these songs guide our study of Scripture. By exploring the songs of Advent and Christmas, we may come to appreciate more deeply the biblical themes of the season.

This week we consider the Advent hymn "O Come, O Come, Emmanuel." This ancient hymn ushers in the Advent season for many Christians who gather

> Do you have a favorite Christmas hymn? What makes this hymn meaningful to your celebration of the birth of Christ?

for worship on the first Sunday of Advent. The hymn is based on a series of Latin antiphons (chanted responses) that probably date from the sixth or seventh century, which the early church sang during the week leading up to Christmas Day. These seven "O Antiphons" are recited or chanted before the *Magnificat* (the Song of Mary, Lk 1:46-55) at evening prayer during the week leading up to Christmas Eve.

By the ninth century, these antiphons were being sung each day leading up to Christmas, but they were not all sung together. Perhaps around the twelfth century, five of them were put together and sung, along with the refrain, "Rejoice! Rejoice! Emmanuel shall come to thee, O Israel." This collection of the antiphons into one musical arrangement is the origin of the hymn we find in our hymnals. However, the tune to which we usually sing this hymn, *"Veni Immanuel,"* was not associated with it until 1854. In that year, John Mason Neale revised his earlier English translation of the Latin text and set it to this music.

Taking time to acknowledge the lasting strength of strong hymn texts—and their enduring message of hope—is an important way for us to prepare for the celebration of Christmas. God's promise that the fulfillment of our hope is approaching resounds once again in the anticipation that Advent proclaims. The witness of God's promise is a story that took centuries to unfold. It began with the Old Testament prophets and continues through the ages through the testimony of the people of God. In a season of rushing, we would do well not to rush to the Nativity. Rather, we should take time to ponder why we and our world so needed the birth of God's Son.

Studying

Perhaps there is not a more tragic figure among the prophets of Israel than Jeremiah. He lived in trying times and had a sensitive and uncompromising character. These circumstances, along with his "divine compulsion to speak out, and his almost total rejection by his people," combined to produce his anguished career (West, 372).

One of Jeremiah's major preoccupations was "the problem of why Israel had failed so miserably in her covenant obligations and what could be done for a people that showed themselves repeatedly incapable of a constant affection for [God's] good purposes" (West, 372–73). West concludes in his commentary that Jeremiah saw that the difficulty was "essentially one of the stubborn human will" (373).

The context for our selected text is Jeremiah 32–33, which is set during Jeremiah's imprisonment (Fretheim, 453). The message of chapter 33 represents a word from the Lord that came to Jeremiah "a second time" (33:1) while he was still imprisoned by King Zedekiah. He was being held in the "court of the guard that was in the palace of the king" (v. 32:2), mainly because he had delivered a prophecy from God that was not pleasing to the ears of the government. Jeremiah's message—the Babylonians are coming so we might as well surrender—was considered traitorous.

His words reveal a fundamental irony: "God's words about freedom and spaciousness are voiced in the midst of restriction and confinement" (Fretheim, 471). Thus Jeremiah's personal situation parallels both the current political situation and the promised outcome for the people of Judah. The exiles are meant to hear these prophetic words of restoration and freedom during a time when they are confined and restricted. Jeremiah's prophecies point forward. They challenge the hearers to listen for something beyond their present circumstances, yet at the same time acknowledge the reality of these circumstances. Jeremiah challenges the people to be realistic about the nature of current events and, more importantly, their own responsibility in creating these present negative circumstances.

At the center of this text is Jeremiah's expectation of a "righteous Branch" springing up for David (Jer 33:15). The prophet also speaks of this "Branch" in 23:5-6. But Jeremiah was not the first to use this imagery in speaking of David's promised heir. Isaiah 11:1 proclaims, "A shoot shall come out from the stump of Jesse, and a branch shall grow out of his roots" (see also Isa 53:12).

After the time of Jeremiah, Zechariah applied this imagery to Zerubbabel, whom he apparently hoped would be a David-like deliverer of the people (see Zech 3:8; 6:12-13). This imagery is also incorporated into one of the "O Antiphons" that lies behind the text of "O Come, O Come, Emmanuel":

> O Flower of Jesse's stem,
> you have been raised up as a sign for all peoples;
> kings stand silent in your presence;
> the nations bow down in worship before you.
> Come, let nothing keep you from coming to our aid.

For Jeremiah, a righteous king and a restored Zion cannot alone meet God's demand for faithfulness. Jeremiah had already "witnessed the failure of the best of Judah's kings to stave off disaster" (West, 373). Israel qualifying for a renewed covenant required "nothing short of a renovation of heart," yet Israel had proven itself incapable of achieving it (West, 373).

The new covenant God intended to make would depend not upon external codes and reforms, but upon a change of the will from within. The people would, in effect, come to desire what God desires (West, 373).

According to West, even though Jeremiah emphasizes the individual dimension of the people changing from within, this emphasis does not remove the responsibility for the corporate body to continue in its covenantal responsibilities. Jeremiah does not envision a private religious experience of the individual in isolation from the group. Rather, he has in mind a new community of the faithful that God will create (West, 373).

Jeremiah's vision is more than idealism. Judah's change in fortune was something he anticipated would happen in history and not merely in the spiritual imaginations of the people. When the prophet spoke of returning from exile, rebuilding the land, and restoring Israel and Judah, he meant these things literally (West, 373).

This message of a restored land and a new city is in keeping with a New Testament theme (Fretheim, 474). Rather than being merely a city rebuilt on the ruins of the old one, the promised restoration is, in fact, to be a new creation. Significantly, this new city is earthly. It is not a heavenly, life-after-death place of residence. It is a gift, come down from the divine to earth (Fretheim, 474).

The restoration of Jerusalem is Jeremiah's primary concern. It is the city of Jerusalem that will live in safety, which is different from what the earlier oracle states in chapter 23. Furthermore, 23:6 states that the Davidic king will be called "the LORD is our righteousness," whereas in 33:16, it is not the king but the entire city of Jerusalem that is called by this name. This change shifts the message from a personal role of leadership and responsibility to one of the whole people, who will enjoy a corporate role of restoration, leadership, and responsibility.

What are some examples of the celebration of lust or gluttony in American entertainment or advertising?

Understanding

Jeremiah was focused on the reformation of individuals from the inside out. The inner being of men and women was fundamental. King Josiah had outlined reforms of the religious system, the institution. But what Jeremiah proclaimed stood in strong contrast to these types of reform. Fixing systems, restructuring organizations, and even changing personnel are the usual first attempts at reform. How different it is for individuals to look inward to change their own hearts and resolve to make personal changes in their lives. Look within, Jeremiah challenges, and make personal changes—rethink your approach, reconsider your motivations and actions—before setting out to change what others are doing.

According to Jeremiah 1:2, Jeremiah began his ministry during the thirteenth year of King Josiah (c. 627 BC), a king remembered for his sweeping religious reforms.

During this season we may perhaps remark many times about the increased hustle and bustle and lament about how early "Christmas" starts in the retail world, from decorations being placed just after Halloween to commercials airing in early

November. We may even complain about insurmountable forces that seem to work against us, taking Christmas away. We may be inclined to claim an attack upon our faith if retail clerks don't wish their customers "Merry Christmas" (Reese, 5). If we are reading Jeremiah, however, our preparations, our faith, and our stability of focus will come from within. Reese comments, "I hope my spirituality doesn't depend on my ability to hear Christmas carols at Wal-Mart" (5). The richness of our experience during this season of preparation for the coming of Emmanuel depends more on our inward preparations and the actions they inspire than on external forces.

Therefore, remember. Remember the God of our ancestors. Remember what God has promised and know that God will come, sending a leader, one who will serve with righteousness and justice. The refrain of "O Come, O Come, Emmanuel" echoes the prophecy that Jeremiah has offered. The promised one is coming, prepare to rejoice: "Rejoice! Rejoice! Emmanuel shall come to thee."

What About Me?

• *Consider the opportunity you may have to be a voice of hope to others.* How might you offer hope or consolation to someone this season? Who do you know that needs to hear the promise of God that ransom, release, and restoration will come? How can you be a presence and example of this claim of faith to someone without using words?

• *Take the time to absorb the season.* Advent is a season of preparation and anticipation of Christmas. So much that surrounds us in this season creates an atmosphere of hurriedness for getting gifts, making plans, and checking off lists. Take time to stop and absorb the moments of worship and the melodies of the songs of the season.

• *The Advent promise is that God will enter our world to bring restoration and wholeness.* What is your world like right now? Are there any fragmented areas of your world and your life? How might God's entering into this world affect you—and those around you?

• *What changes would you like to see in your life?* Jeremiah asks us to consider first looking inward with honest reflection at our lives. Instead of expecting everything around us to change, he encourages us to change from within. Are there mistakes that need to be acknowledged? Do we have habits that need to be reconsidered? What first steps might we identify? Remember that it is with God's presence that we are able to know new beginnings. Trust in this Advent promise.

Resources

Terence E. Fretheim, *Jeremiah*, Smyth & Helwys Bible Commentary (Macon GA: Smyth & Helwys, 2002).

The Penguin Book of Carols, ed. Ian Bradley (London: Penguin, 1999).

Stephen Reese, *Hope for the Thinking Christian: Seeking a Path of Faith through Everyday Life* (Macon GA: Smyth & Helwys, 2010).

William Saunders "What Are the 'O Antiphons'?" <http://www.catholiceducation.org/articles/religion/re0374.html>.

James King West, *Introduction to the Old Testament*, 2nd ed. (New York: Macmillan, 1981).

Until the Son of God Appears

Jeremiah 33:14-16

Introduction

I know of a church that places a large, white candle on the communion table the first Sunday of Advent. That in itself is not unusual. But this particular candle is encircled by barbed wired. The symbolism of the barbed-wire candle is obvious: light has come into the world, but it is still encircled by evil.

On the Christian calendar, we begin a new year today. The Christian year starts on the first Sunday of Advent, when it is beginning to get dark earlier than any other time of the year. In the middle of winter, when it is dark and cold, we Christians light special candles to remind ourselves that a light has come into the world, a light that shines in the midst of darkness. We begin a new Christian year by lighting candles and celebrating the coming of One who declared himself to be the light of the world.

When Jeremiah wrote the prophecy that bears his name, he was addressing people who were living in darkness. The Babylonian Empire had conquered Judah, their beloved home-land. Many Jews had been carried off to Babylon. Jeremiah was writing to these people in exile, trying to give them hope, trying to help them see the candle in their barbed-wire existence.

In our verses for this week, the prophet tries to get them to lift their eyes to the future and see the good things God has in store for them. There is coming a day, Jeremiah says, when God will fulfill the promises he made to Israel and Judah. He will raise up one from the line of David who will execute justice and right-eousness in the land. There is coming a day, he says, when Judah will be saved, and Jerusalem will be safe. This one who is coming will be known as the Righteous One.

In the darkness of exile and despair, Jeremiah tried to light a candle of hope. Don't give up, he pleaded. God is not through with you yet. Keep trusting. Keep being faithful. Even in the darkness, keep believing in a good God.

Jeremiah's words of hope did three things for the people of Judah, which we need to know and claim in our own experience.

Light in a Dark World

First, Jeremiah was trying to shine light in a dark world. We can hardly imagine what it would be like to be uprooted from our home, removed from our job, separated from our family and friends, and hauled off to a foreign country. But that is what happened to the people of Judah. It must have been a dark, depressing experience. Jeremiah tried desperately to provide a little light in that darkness. The promise of One who would make things right was intended to keep those people from despair.

Although we can't fully identify with the trauma of being carried off into exile, most of us have no trouble at all relating to the concept of living in darkness. We, too, have had times of trouble, times when we felt God let us down, times when we suffered and felt totally alone. Typically, we don't share these dark experiences publicly; we just endure them privately. But they are real, and they make us miserable.

For years, our family sent an annual Christmas letter to our friends. We gave a brief synopsis of each family member. From reading this letter, you would believe we never had a single problem that year. We wrote about babies born, books published, trips taken, and awards won. And what we wrote was the truth. That baby *was* born, that book *was* published, that trip *was* taken, and that award *was* won. But there was a darker side to every year, a side we left unreported. Christmas, after all, is about light, and we didn't want to depress people with our darkness.

But the darkness was there. And it is there for most of the people you will be teaching this week. As you teach, you can do what Jeremiah did for the people of Judah: put some light in their darkness. You get to say that God has kept his promise. The

Righteous One has come. Jesus has not only lived an exemplary life to show us how to live, he has died for our sins to fill us with gratitude and joy.

This Sunday, and throughout the Advent season, we celebrate the Light of the World who shines in our personal darkness and remember that the darkness cannot overcome that Light (Jn 1:5).

The Faithfulness of God

Second, Jeremiah reminded them of the faithfulness of God. His promise of the coming Righteous One was a way of assuring those disconsolate people that, contrary to what they might feel, God was still working in their midst. God was still sovereign over their lives.

The problem for the people of Judah—and for us—is that God's help is usually invisible. The writer H. G. Wells once described God as an ever-absent help in time of trouble, and there are days when we might agree. If God is faithful, why don't we receive tangible help? Where is the healing? Where is the peace? Where is the answer to our prayer?

In my own understanding of God's faithfulness, I've been helped by Robert Capon's distinction between two kinds of help. In his book *The Third Peacock* (Garden City NJ: Doubleday, 1972), he says there is "mechanical help" and there is "personal help."

Mechanical help "fixes" a problem. It changes things, and the results are obvious. When we pray, it is mechanical help we nearly always seek. We want God to fix things, give us miracles, rescue us from a bad situation, heal the sickness, or bring peace to our conflict. We want God to do something tangible, and we're confused and disappointed when we don't get our wish.

But there is also personal help, Capon says. It's the kind of help that gives us hope, peace, and maybe even joy. Though we may not always like it, it seems that this is usually the kind of help God chooses to give us. It is the kind of help displayed when Jesus died on the cross:

> When the invisible hand that holds the stars finally does its triumphant restoring thing, it does nothing at all but hang there and bleed. That may well be help; but it is not the Band-Aid creation expected on the basis of mechanical analogies. The

only way it makes sense is when it is seen as personal: When we are helpless, there he is. He doesn't start your stalled car for you; he comes and sits with you in the snowbank. You can object that he should have made a world in which cars don't stall; but you can't complain he doesn't stick by his customers. (Capon, 91-92)

In our darkness, God comes to sit beside us. He is Immanuel, "God with us," giving us hope, peace, joy, and love, and as we light our candles this Advent season, we celebrate the personal help God has given us in the past—and will continue to give us in the future.

Good and Evil

Third, Jeremiah asserted that good would eventually defeat evil. The people of Judah had to be wondering if evil had triumphed. All of the evidence indicated that was the case. The Babylonians had conquered them, their world had been overturned, and the future had been swallowed by despair. But Jeremiah said that was not the case at all. In fact, God was going to send One who would administer justice and righteousness. The final curtain had not fallen yet, and good was going to defeat evil after all.

That is still hard to believe, and on some days, believing takes all of the faith we can muster. The headlines in the newspaper this morning told me about a horrifying incident of child abuse, a senseless murder in our city, and several local accidents that took the lives of innocent people. Then there was the usual fare about economic woes, political bickering, and corporate greed. If all we had to go by was news from the morning paper, we might be forced to admit that evil had indeed conquered the world.

But with faith the size of a mustard seed, we dare to say that the story is not over yet. God is alive and well and sovereign over the world. And someday there will be justice and righteousness in the land. We also know we must do our little part in making that happen. Establishing the kingdom of God on earth was the passion of Jesus' life, and it is supposed to be the passion of his followers as well.

Last year, I remember following the progress of my favorite college football team, the Baylor Bears. When a particular game wasn't televised, I had to be content with occasional score updates while I watched another game. Early in the fourth quarter of a memorable game, the Bears were losing 24-3 against a team they were supposed to whip handily. Frustrated, I cut off the television and started doing other things. But I was fretting and fuming about the Bears' defeat.

A few hours later, I flipped on the television and saw a score scroll along the bottom of the screen that I thought said Baylor had won 31-30. Curious and hopeful, I called my son to get the scoop on the game. It was true, he assured me. The Bears scored three touchdowns in the final quarter, and then won the game in overtime. They had snatched victory from the jaws of defeat. The moral of the story, I suppose, is "it ain't over 'til it's over."

In effect, this is Jeremiah's message to those exiles in Babylon. He was telling them, "You might think the game is over. You might think evil has won. You might be fretting and fuming about your miserable fate. But don't give up. Check the score later, and you'll see that good overcame evil. You'll see that God won after all."

Conclusion

In the New Testament, we have two accounts of the birth of Jesus—one in Matthew and one in Luke.

Luke's account of Jesus' birth is full of joy and gladness. He has everybody singing: Zechariah, Mary, the angels, and Simeon all sing in Luke's gospel. Most of the joyful images we have of Jesus' birth are from Luke. He's the one who inspires our songs and fills our heads and hearts with angels, shepherds, Mary, Joseph, and the baby.

Matthew also gives us a version of Jesus' birth, but it is considerably darker. Matthew has no angels, no shepherds, and nobody singing. In Matthew's version of the story, Joseph is concerned that his wife is already great with child, Herod threatens the safety of the holy family, the Magi take the long way home to avoid facing the crazy king, and Joseph and Mary are afraid to go home, too. Matthew's Christmas story is full of darkness and fear. In Matthew's Christmas story, the light is there, but the barbed wire is there as well. Jesus is born, but he is born into a barbed-wire kind of world.

The people of Judah in Jeremiah's day would have had no trouble seeing the barbed wire. The danger for them was that they would see only the barbed wire. Stuck in the trauma of exile, they had a hard time seeing the candle. Where was God in this darkness? Where was hope in this hopeless situation?

Jeremiah and some of the other prophets tried to say a positive word in this negative situation. The messianic prophecies were intended to give light in a dark world, remind the people of the faithfulness of God, and assure the people that good would eventually triumph over evil. As we begin the Advent season this Sunday, we have the opportunity to celebrate those three truths.

The first verse and chorus of "O Come, O Come, Emmanuel" provide a fitting synopsis of our verses in Jeremiah and a fitting conclusion to the lesson:

O come, O come, Emmanuel, and ransom captive Israel,
That mourns in lonely exile here, until the Son of God appear.
Rejoice! Rejoice! Emmanuel shall come to thee, O Israel!

Notes

Notes

2

HAIL THE
INCARNATE DEITY

Isaiah 7:14; Matthew 1:22-23;
Luke 1:26-28; John 1:14

Central Question

Where do I experience God's revelation in human form?

Scripture

Isaiah 7:14 14 Therefore the LORD himself will give you a sign. Look, the young woman is with child and shall bear a son, and shall name him Immanuel.

Matthew 1:22-23 22 All this took place to fulfill what had been spoken by the Lord through the prophet: 23 "Look, the virgin shall conceive and bear a son, and they shall name him Emmanuel," which means, "God is with us."

Luke 1:26-28 26 In the sixth month the angel Gabriel was sent by God to a town in Galilee called Nazareth, 27 to a virgin engaged to a man whose name was Joseph, of the house of David. The virgin's name was Mary. 28 And he came to her and said, "Greetings, favored one! The Lord is with you."

John 1:14 14 And the Word became flesh and lived among us, and we have seen his glory, the glory as of a father's only son, full of grace and truth.

Reflecting

Today's carol was written by Charles Wesley for Christmas Day 1739 and was originally known as "Hark How All the Welkin Rings." The lyrics and tune to which we sing it today were not combined until over 100 years later, in the 1850s.

It is not unusual for hymn texts to be set to different tunes in different times and places. What makes this particular combination so interesting, though, is the contrary purposes of the text and the tune with which we associate it today. Wesley's carol is rich with biblical and theological references. But his original poem, ten verses of four lines each, experienced revisions and omissions over time that might not have pleased him. Further, the tune with which it is paired would have surprised and perhaps even shocked its author. Felix Mendelssohn wrote this tune for the 400th anniversary of the invention of printing. Here is what Mendelssohn himself said of this tune:

> I think there ought to be other words to No. 2. If the right ones are hit at, I am sure the piece will be liked very much by the singers and the hearers, but it will never do to sacred words. There must be a national and merry subject found out, something to which the soldier-like and buxom motion of the piece has some relation, and the words must express something gay and popular as the music tries to do it. (*The Penguin Book of Carols*, 130)

W. H. Cummings, organist of Waltham Abbey parish church in Essex, England, brought text and tune together. A revised text combined with a tune never intended for sacred words "have combined to produce one of the most popular hymns in the English language" (*The Penguin Book of Carols*, 130).

Studying

Wesley's carol "Hark! the Herald Angels Sing" richly proclaims the theological meaning of Jesus' birth. In particular, consider the lines,

The more accurate rendering of the Hebrew word is "Immanuel." The form "Emmanuel" comes to us by way of Greek and Latin.

"Pleased as man with man to dwell, Jesus our Immanuel."
Matthew links the meaning of Jesus' birth with Isaiah 7:14,
thus the Immanuel quotation "promises such days for God's
people as they have never known before" (Albright and Mann, lv).
According to Witherington, "Immanuel" refers to "a throne name
for a king rather than a personal name" (47). Jesus will be called a
"living presence of God with God's people" (Witherington, 47).
Here, we see in the beginning of the Gospel of Matthew what is
found in the pronouncement of Jesus, the risen Christ, in
Matthew 28:20: "I am with you always."

In its original context, Isaiah's prophecy is a sign that brings
both warning and hope. He acknowledges the threat of the
rapidly expanding Assyrian Empire. Even so, the prophet draws
attention to a woman who will soon give birth to a son, a sign of
hope in spite of the political uncertainty. Immanuel, meaning
God is with us, "would thereby serve as an assurance that there
was nothing to fear from those who now threatened Judah"
(Clements, 88). Isaiah warns of impending consequences if the
king does not accept it, yet he perhaps "still hoped to persuade
Ahaz with his prophetic message" (Clements, 88).

In Matthew 1:22-23, the Gospel writer draws from the
Scriptures for confirmation of "the truth or significance of
something he is reporting" (Hare, 95). He quotes Isaiah 7:14 to
support his claims about Mary's miraculous conception. The
Hebrew version of this verse, and the Greek version Matthew
quotes, are slightly different. The Greek translation reads, "the
virgin," while in Hebrew the word refers to a young woman more
generally; she might be either married or unmarried. In Isaiah, in
Hebrew, the context "does not suggest a miraculous birth" (Hare,
95). Even so, Christian belief in the virginal conception of Jesus
doesn't hang on Isaiah 7:14. In Luke's birth narrative, where
Isaiah's prophecy is never mentioned, there is a clear affirmation
of Mary's virginity.

The Greek translation of Isaiah 7:14 comes from a time
(third and second century BC) when Israel's longing for a coming
deliverer was reaching a fever pitch and reflects a pre-Christian
messianic interpretation of Isaiah's prophecy. This understanding of the text likely had significance for Matthew and his

community. Because of their reflection on the significance of Jesus' birth, the early Christians came to read Isaiah 7:14 in this new light (Witherington, 43). In particular, they were no doubt drawn to the title "Immanuel," which in Hebrew means "God with us."

This name is a divine promise "that God will be with the nation in the midst of international crises" (Hare, 97). Matthew gives evidence that the Christian community saw not only this understanding, "but also the assurance that, with the birth of Jesus, God had uniquely invaded history and was now truly with us" (Cate, 403). The assurance that we are not alone transcends the centuries, from Isaiah's original proclamation, to the angel's announcement, to our present Advent anticipation. God, who created us in God's image, who lived and died as one of us, is with us even now, in our time of need, of life, and of Christmas. We anticipate this mysterious truth to be real in our lives and we celebrate this miraculous presence.

Only two Gospels—Matthew and Luke—have birth narratives. But the significance of Jesus coming into the world is also explored in the first 18 verses of John's Gospel, referred to as the Prologue. This passage "presents a birth narrative unique for the ways in which it speaks in poetic language about God, creation, Word, light and darkness, and Jesus Christ" (Hedahl, 188). Although not a narrative, in the technical sense, of the story of Jesus' birth, John provides a lasting image of Jesus' coming and his presence with us. John describes the mystery of this good news: the very "Word [that] was with God" in the beginning (Jn 1:1) has now "become flesh in Jesus and 'pitched his tent' among us" (Culpepper, 191).

Culpepper points out that the opening of John's Gospel "declares not what the first disciples saw and heard, but what they later come to understand" (191). Like John's Prologue, Wesley's carol calls Christians to sing what we have come to understand about Jesus Christ. The call to "hail the incarnate Deity" rings out in our voices as we echo what John penned at the beginning of his Gospel. Jesus, the Word

What signs do you see of God being with us today? What does it mean if there are no clear signs of God's presence?

that was God and was with God from the beginning, has now become flesh—human—and resides with us.

Understanding

The prophecy of Isaiah comes to us in Advent. As it does, Immanuel, this God-with-us message of hope, becomes a sign that "raises the question of how God enters and acts within the world of time and space" (Saliers, 76). It is as true now as it was centuries ago that "in complicated times—politically, socially, economically—the yearning for some sign of promise and hope in the form of a new leader is still very much with us" (Saliers, 76). This sign of Immanuel also reveals "the gap between what the world is and what it ought to be" (Saliers, 76). During Advent we acknowledge this gap once again and call ourselves to remember that though the risen Christ is ever present, we still live in a world in need of redemption and restoration. Saliers continues, "Living into a future that has not yet come to be is living into the unexpected" (78). Advent calls us to do so with a perspective of hopeful expectation.

> What indications do you see around you that the world is not yet what it ought to be? What can you do this Advent season to bring a little bit more of God's kingdom into the world?

Our Advent preparations help us remember the promise that comes to God's servants. We rediscover this promise for the significance it held for God's people in the past as well as the significance it has for us today. As Saliers says, "The promise of a Messiah is grounded in God's intention to restore us and to transform the world as we have come to make it into our own image" (78). As our Advent preparations continue, we are encouraged to trust the promise that God is with us.

What About Me?

• *God says, "I will be with you."* This is one of the recurring themes through all of Scripture. Advent reminds us that God will be present in all of our living. This is a promise we can trust. Where in our lives do we most need God to be present with us?

• *A living presence of God.* Witherington uses the phrase "a living presence of God" to describe Jesus. When you consider that God has become a living presence, in human form, likeness, and understanding, with and among the people God created and loves, how does this influence your expectations about how God operates in our world?

• *Grow deeper in your understanding of the Christmas message.* Recall your impressions and understandings of the story of Jesus' birth when you were a child. What do you remember being emphasized? What Scripture passages, either Old Testament or New Testament, do you recall being read? How has your understanding of the Christmas message developed as you have grown and matured? How has your understanding deepened and been enriched?

Resources

W. F. Albright and C. S. Mann, *Matthew*, The Anchor Bible (New York: Doubleday, 1971).

Robert L. Cate, "Immanuel," *Mercer Dictionary of the Bible*, ed. Watson E. Mills et al. (Macon GA: Mercer University Press, 1990).

R. E. Clements. *Isaiah 1–19*, New Century Bible Commentary (Grand Rapids MI: Eerdmans, 1980).

R. Alan Culpepper, "John 1:(1-9) 10-18," *Feasting on the Word, Year A*, vol. 1, ed. David L. Bartlett and Barbara Brown Taylor (Louisville KY: Westminster/John Knox, 2010).

Douglas R. A. Hare, "Matthew 1:18-25," *Feasting on the Word, Year A*, vol. 1, ed. David L. Bartlett and Barbara Brown Taylor (Louisville KY: Westminster/John Knox, 2010).

Susan Hedahl, "John 1:(1-9) 10-18," *Feasting on the Word, Year A*, vol. 1, ed. David L. Bartlett and Barbara Brown Taylor (Louisville KY: Westminster/John Knox, 2010).

The Penguin Book of Carols, ed. Ian Bradley (London: Penguin, 1999).

Don Saliers, "Isaiah 7:10-16," *Feasting on the Word, Year A*, vol. 1, ed. David L. Bartlett and Barbara Brown Taylor (Louisville KY: Westminster/John Knox, 2010).

Ben Witherington III, , Smyth & Helwys Bible Commentary (Macon GA: Smyth & Helwys, 2006).

Hail the Incarnate Deity

Isaiah 7:14; Matthew 1:22-23;
Luke 1:26-28; John 1:14

Introduction

A noted preacher once described the first Christmas as "the day God walked down the stairs of heaven with a baby in his arms."

All four of our passages this week focus on that truth, that God revealed himself through a baby born in Bethlehem. Famously, Isaiah 7:14 predicts the coming of Immanuel, "God with us." The verses from Matthew allude to that verse from Isaiah. The Luke passage tells us of Mary's call by the angel Gabriel. Finally, John 1:14 tells us that God became flesh and lived among us so we could behold his glory. If we don't get it in Isaiah, surely we'll get it by the time we get to John: God became visible in the person of Jesus. That baby born in Bethlehem was the incarnate Deity.

These verses give us an opportunity to reflect on the up-close-and-personal nature of the Christian faith—how God chose to become human, how Jesus chose to be personal in his ministry, and how we are to be personal as we relate to the people around us. As we probe these verses, let's think about what God did, what Jesus did, and what we are called to do.

What God Did

God actually did more than walk down the stairs of heaven with a baby in his arms. When God sent Jesus into the world, he gave us a picture of himself. As Paul says in his letter to the Colossians, Jesus "is the image of the invisible God" (1:15) and "in him all the fullness of God was pleased to dwell" (1:19). If you've seen Jesus, you've seen God.

That is an astonishing and surprising piece of news. Of all of the ways God could have revealed himself, he did it like this? As a baby in a bed of straw? As a child growing up in a family in Nazareth? As a young teacher who alienated the religious leaders of his day? As a friend of outcasts and sinners? As a common criminal crucified between two thieves? This is how God chose to reveal himself?

You would think the God of the universe would have done something more dramatic and obvious, like thundering divine edicts from heaven, writing a divine message in the stars, or having the waves roar a divine sermon from the ocean. But God chose instead to become flesh as a baby in Bethlehem and live among us so humanity could see him up close and personal.

That truth has at least two practical implications for us. First, it means that we can know some important things about the character of God. We're not completely in the dark. We have the picture on the puzzle box, as it were, so we know what God looks like. To the all-important question, "What is God like?" we have a specific answer: God is like Jesus.

Second, it means we need to look long and hard at Jesus. If it is really true that Jesus is "the image of the invisible God," we need to look at that image very closely because the more we know about Jesus the better we understand God. As we learn about Jesus—who he was, what he said and did, and how he related to people—we come to a clearer understanding of God.

With that thought lingering in our minds, let's turn our attention to what Jesus did when he walked upon the earth and revealed God to us.

What Jesus Did

When I read the Gospels, I can almost feel the frustration of Jesus' disciples. They thought he was the promised Messiah, that he would usher in a new reign of pomp and power for Israel, and that they would receive important positions in his new regime. They just knew that Jesus would do what any respectable Messiah would do: launch a movement, pull strings, win battles, sway voters, win debates, raise money, and all of the other things successful politicians did.

And what did Jesus do? He focused on specific people, most of them the kind of people who could not possibly advance his campaign. He stopped and talked to blind Bartimaeus. He conversed with the woman at the well. He took little children on his lap and gave them his undivided attention. He had dinner with a little crook named Zaccheus. And he rejected a fine, upstanding potential follower like the rich, young ruler.

It must have seemed to his followers that Jesus alienated the people who could help him most and loved the people who could do nothing to advance his cause.

But Jesus was on a completely different wavelength from that of his disciples, and they seemingly didn't understand him until he died. They thought he would focus on crowds, but he was interested in individual people. They thought he was intent on building a political kingdom where power was paramount, but he was interested in building a spiritual kingdom where compassion was the key. They thought he would mesmerize the masses, but he came to build a kingdom of love one person at a time.

It is not hard at all to understand their frustration. How can you impress society when you hang out with riffraff? How can you build a powerful kingdom when you spend all of your time with powerless people? How long will it take to change the world if you go about it one person at a time? From the disciples' perspective, Jesus was like no Messiah they had ever envisioned. He desperately needed a course in Messiah 101.

What We Are Called to Do

Before we throw too many stones at those misguided disciples, though, let us at least admit that, some 2,000 years later, we don't understand Jesus, either. His way still seems strange, inefficient, and ineffective. This business of being personal and paying attention to individual people seems like a poor way to launch a worldwide movement. No self-respecting politician could get elected following that approach.

Let's also give the disciples credit since they did eventually "get it" and become proponents of the strange kingdom of love

Jesus established. When you read the writings of people such as Peter and John, you realize they did come around to Jesus' way of thinking and encouraged the early church to embrace it.

Listen, for example, to John: "We know love by this, that he laid down his life for us—and we ought to lay down our lives for one another. How does God's love abide in anyone who has the world's goods and sees a brother or sister in need and yet refuses help? Little children, let us love, not in word or speech, but in truth and action" (1 Jn 3:16-18).

I would remind you that that is the same John who, years earlier, had asked Jesus to let him and his brother James be first and second in Jesus' new regime. John had come a long way in his understanding of who Jesus was and what Jesus came to do. He embraced Jesus' personal style of relationships, and those verses in 1 John spell out that style very clearly. They remind us that Jesus' way of loving individual people has three characteristics.

First, love sees. Love sees that we have "the world's goods" and plenty to share. Love also sees our brothers and sisters in need and pays attention to them. The person who loves the Jesus Way focuses on specific people.

Second, love feels. John raises the possibility that we can see needy people and not be moved to respond. We can see, he says, and refuse to help. Love has an emotional component to it. It is moved to say, "I can't let that happen."

Third, love acts. John says we are to love, not in word or speech, but in truth and action. We see. We feel. And then we act, dispensing food to the hungry, water to the thirsty, clothes to the naked, homes to the homeless, and focused attention on the variety of hurts people have.

When we follow John's progression, though, we see how difficult the Jesus Way is. The "love cycle" can break down anywhere along the way. First, it is possible not to see, to be so focused on our own lives we don't even notice the people around us.

It is also possible to see, but not to feel. We can become so calloused and insensitive that we're not moved by the plight of the people around us.

And then it is possible to see and feel, but not to act. We can see needs, feel sorry for people, yet never get around to doing anything tangible to help them.

Since love can break down anywhere in that cycle, it's easy to see why actually living the Jesus Way is a rarity. Those who see, feel, and act are a small minority. I suppose Jesus would say they are walking a narrow road.

Jesus' kind of love is never general; it is always specific. We might declare that we love children, but unless we love little Sarah with the runny nose and missing front tooth, we don't know what love is. We might say we love old people, but unless we love Mrs. Franklin wrapped up in the quilt over there in the rocking chair, we don't really know what love is. Love sees specific people, feels their joys and sorrows, and acts to make a difference in their lives.

To their credit, John and the other early disciples eventually understood the strategy of Jesus. They realized that his focused attention on individual people was the essential ingredient in this strange, new kingdom he came to build. Had Jesus come to build a political kingdom of might and power, individual acts of love directed at individual people would have been useless. But since he came to build a spiritual kingdom of love and joy, individual acts of love directed at individual people were the indispensable nails that built it and held it together.

We can only hope and pray that we understand and embrace Jesus' strategy, too.

Conclusion

Our verses for this week draw our attention to the focused love of God and the way Jesus embodied that kind of love in his life and ministry. God transcended generalities and particularized his love by becoming one of us. Jesus particularized his love by seeking out individual people and meeting their needs. And now we are to particularize our love, too, and see, feel, and act so that individual people around us know that someone cares.

In his book *Love in Four Dimensions* (Nashville TN: Broadman, 1982), William Hull wrote,

While we need not minimize the threat of atomic annihilation, its destruction for many would be mercifully swift, whereas death from not being loved is always slow and painful. No bomb has been invented that can inflict as much cruelty on the vital core of our being as the blight of feeling that no one cares. (70)

It is time for those of us who follow Jesus to start thinking small, narrow our focus, love a few people lavishly, serve our churches, do a good job at work, and give our money to help build God's kingdom. In short, it's time for us to quit loving "the world" and start loving individual people. Contrary to what we sometimes feel, we have not been given too much to do; we just have to do a few things with God's kind of focused love.

The second stanza of "Hark! the Herald Angels Sing" gives us a clear synopsis of our verses for this week:

Christ, by highest heav'n adored, Christ the everlasting Lord;
Late in time, behold him come, offspring of a virgin's womb.
Veiled in flesh the Godhead see, hail the incarnate Deity!
Pleased as man with men to dwell, Jesus our Immanuel.

Immanuel has come—not only to save us from our sins, but also to show us how we are supposed to live and love.

Notes

Notes

3

OF THE FATHER'S LOVE BEGOTTEN

Isaiah 12:2-6

Central Question

How is Jesus the evidence of God's eternal love?

Scripture

Isaiah 12:2-6 2 Surely God is my salvation; I will trust, and will not be afraid, for the LORD GOD is my strength and my might; he has become my salvation. 3 With joy you will draw water from the wells of salvation. 4 And you will say in that day: Give thanks to the LORD, call on his name; make known his deeds among the nations; proclaim that his name is exalted. 5 Sing praises to the LORD, for he has done gloriously; let this be known in all the earth. 6 Shout aloud and sing for joy, O royal Zion, for great in your midst is the Holy One of Israel.

Reflecting

Folks who ask to "sing the old hymns" in church probably don't have in mind hymns as old as the carol "Of the Father's Love Begotten." The author of this poem was Aurelius Clemens Prudentius (AD 349–410), a lawyer and provincial governor in Roman Spain who later retired from public life to follow a path of strict religious discipline.

The poem's original text has been translated numerous times over the centuries. Various portions of the poem were used in worship in the ninth and eleventh centuries, although very few hymnals reproduced the text in its entirety or in its original form.

Furthermore, some editors have "cherry-picked what they consider the best bits of these various translations and strung them together" (*The Penguin Book of Carols*, 236). As a result, this hymn text has enjoyed a very long life, mirroring the message that it carries of the eternal nature of God's love and the ongoing story of the birth of this love in the Christ child.

The hymn "speaks so majestically and sonorously about Christ in all his attributes, human and divine" (*The Penguin Book of Carols*, 232). Sung to what is described as a "haunting plainsong melody" (*The Penguin Book of Carols*, 236), this chant-like tune reflects the message of God's eternal love that is embedded in the words of the refrain, "Evermore and evermore."

A different translation of the first line uses the words "will" or "heart" instead of "love." The original Latin word is *corde*, for which "of [the] heart" is actually a more accurate literal translation (*The Penguin Book of Carols*, 233). Insert the word "heart" in the first line: "Of the Father's *heart* begotten." How does this deepen your understanding of the gracious and enduring gift that comes from God?

Studying

Isaiah 12:1-6 has been described as a "song of praise to Yahweh" (Harrelson, 241), a "responsive psalm" (Olson, 297), and "a Song of Thanksgiving which has its closet counterparts in Psalmody" (Clements, 127). This psalm-like passage in the prophet Isaiah's message serves "as a conclusion to the overall message of judgment followed by hope which is to be found in chapters 1–11 of the book" (Clements, 128). Viewed in the full light of the preceding chapters, particularly Isaiah 5–11, the prophet gives this response in reaction to all of the good things God has promised. Even so, Olson notes that it "is not a psalm of praise, extolling God for what is; it is a poem of hope, praising God for what will be in the future" (299). Here, we find our connection to Advent; we, like the Israelites of long ago, are in a period of waiting in which we anticipate God's coming gift of salvation.

Step into the hope that Isaiah proclaims. The prophet gives witness to who God is and will be—"God is my salvation; I will trust, and will not be afraid" (Isa 12:2). These are words of confidence and testimony in the saving power of God. They recognize that it is God who delivers, who is the source of strength and the source of salvation.

Isaiah 12:2 states that "the LORD GOD is my strength and my might." The word translated "might" implies energy or vitality (Clements, 129). This phrase echoes Exodus 15:2 and Psalm 118:14. It was in Exodus 15 that Moses and Miriam led the people in song following their deliverance. Isaiah calls to remembrance the God of salvation in order to inspire a vision for hope of a time when God will once again deliver the people and be their source of strength and salvation. The repetition of this text from Exodus 15:2 links the God who saved their ancestors in the past to the same God at work on their deliverance now. As Hooke notes, this is "the same God who continues to be faithful to God's people, and now brings them home in a second exodus" (Hooke, 298).

Prepare for this day of deliverance, Isaiah says, for you will sing a song of thanksgiving. The present time is dreadful. Judgment has been harsh—and not undeserved. There are consequences for wrongdoing; grace and salvation do not guarantee that we can avoid these consequences. But judgment is not the final word. God will save and restore us. The prophet insists that the people will again sing the praise of God and tell of God's redeeming love. Hooke writes, "God's promise of restoration is so sure that, for the faithful remnant, it is as though it has already happened, and they are compelled to offer thanks in response" (298).

In verse 3 Isaiah uses the imagery of life-giving water. The image of drawing water is "designed to stress the limitless possibilities which Israel will enjoy when the time of its salvation has arrived" (Clements, 129). Many of us in the Western world take purified water for granted. It runs practically free from our taps, and we use it lavishly on our lawns and in our swimming pools (Tull, 249).

How might Israel's preparation for their coming "day of deliverance" compare with the spiritual preparations Christians make during Advent? How are they the same? How are they different?

We must not forget the power and importance that this image communicated to the people in ancient times, in an arid region of the world. Water—and in particular the lack of it—has often shaped history dramatically.

In verse 4 the prophet says, "And you will say in that day: Give thanks to the LORD." A time is coming, he claims, when God's promises will be fulfilled. The people will "draw water from the wells of salvation" (v. 3) and give thanks to God. By noting this future gratitude, Isaiah proclaims God's goodness in the present and encourages the people to tell of God's good deeds. This Advent season, as we await once again the coming of Christ, we need to hear this call to remember and to tell of the good deeds, the saving grace, and the underlying source of strength that is in God.

Verse 5 encourages the people to "sing praises to the LORD." As Clements explains, "Those who have experienced the greatness of God's salvation are pictured as summoning all their fellow Israelites to give the maximum of praise to him" (129). Verse 6, like the rest of the chapter, emphasizes God's presence among the people and "marks a goal of the post-exilic Jewish hope" (Clements, 129).

Chapter 12 concludes the first major section of the book of Isaiah. In this section, the prophecy of Isaiah has pronounced "God's judgment on the people of Judah for their breaking of covenant with God, and for their acts of injustice toward the weakest members of their society" (Hooke, 296). The purpose of our lesson is not to focus on Isaiah's strong warnings in previous chapters. Even so, it is important to keep these warnings in mind to better understand the theological message and devotional power of Isaiah 12. According to Schneider, "Both the story and the God whose anger appears literally to decimate the people should not be forgotten in the relief and praise that flood this brief conclusion" (296). We are meant to assume that Isaiah's hearers have learned their lesson. One of the first things they have learned is "that God's anger always gives way to 'comfort,' a word that in Hebrew literally means the removal of a burden so that a person can breathe freely again" (Hooke, 298). Even when we do not deserve it, grace and forgiveness flow freely from the loving heart of the Father.

Understanding

This passage invites Christians to reconsider some of our assumptions about the Old Testament. We often depict the Hebrew Scriptures as a source of bad news that is answered by the good news of the New Testament. But this passage challenges us to consider "the joyful hope the prophets voiced for the future of life on this side of eternity—the side on which all living persons now find ourselves, the side on which we hope to live in peace throughout our natural lives" (Tull, 251). Echoing the praise of the exodus saga, these verses are written in a future tense. They express praise for a rescue that has not yet occurred. The image is that of "a song sung by slaves who are singing now the songs of their great-grandchildren, far in advance of freedom" (Schneider, 298).

Here, perhaps we can perceive Scripture's continual living nature. It is one thing to read the text in order to understand our ancestors in the faith and the story of how God acted in their lives. It is quite another to hear the Bible's living and active voice in our current situation.

As a sign of the depth of our conviction, it is important to sing God's praises for the sake of our great-grandchildren. We must give testimony in the present to our faith and trust that God will bring salvation. We should give testimony that God has delivered us in the past, acknowledging our former sins and faithlessness. In this way we demonstrate our understanding of how our previous acts of discrimination and injustice do not reflect God's intentions for us or for our world.

The hymn "Of the Father's Love Begotten" speaks of the never-ending love which comes from God. This love creates, redeems, and calls forth our praise. This love came to life in Jesus, "the Babe, the world's Redeemer" who "first revealed his sacred face."

Isaiah's words offer us a model of learning from the past, with an eye toward our present circumstances, so that we may live into a new future. It also offers an excellent opportunity for congregations worshiping during painful seasons of life "to pray with anticipation for the day when spontaneous and heartfelt joy returns, the day of salvation" (Tull, 251). Drawing from Israel's past experience with the God of salvation, Isaiah's words become for us a sign that points to the one whom God has sent, the Alpha and the Omega, the source of "the things that are, that have been and that the future years shall see." In his name we give praise, thanksgiving, and witness to God for God's great love, displayed for us in the sending of God's Son, which endures "evermore and evermore!"

What About Me?

• *God's love is unending.* Where do you find the thread of God's unending love in your life? When have you been blessed by the abundance within God's loving heart? As we remember Jesus as the crowning expression of God's love for us, let us also take time to thank God for the many daily gestures of divine lovingkindness.

• *Prepare to celebrate.* Our circumstances may look bleak at times, but Christmas is coming! God's gift of the Son is ample reason to praise and give thanks. How can we prepare now to celebrate the birth of Jesus nine days from now?

• *Make the connection.* The God we worship and to whom we pray is not only the Father of our Savior Jesus Christ, but also the God of the Hebrews, who led this oppressed people to freedom. How often do we recognize that the God we call upon and worship is the same one who heard the cries of the slaves in Egypt and who spoke through the prophet Isaiah?

• *Be a witness to the generations that will follow.* The actions we take in demonstrating our faith, including our confessions, acknowledgements of God's work in our lives, and offerings we make, are among the important ways we express our faith to the younger people who are with us. The actions our congregations take bear witness to what we *actually* believe far more powerfully than what we merely *say* we believe.

Resources

R. E. Clements, *Isaiah 1-39*, New Century Bible Commentary (Grand Rapids MI: Eerdmans, 1980).

Walter Harrelson, *Interpreting the Old Testament* (New York: Holt, Rinehart and Winston, 1964).

Ruthanna Hooke, "Isaiah 12," *Feasting on the Word, Year C*, vol. 4, ed. David L. Bartlett and Barbara Brown Taylor (Louisville KY: Westminster/John Knox, 2010).

Susan K. Olson, "Isaiah 12," *Feasting on the Word, Year C*, vol. 4, ed. David L. Bartlett and Barbara Brown Taylor (Louisville KY: Westminster/John Knox, 2010).

The Penguin Book of Carols, ed. Ian Bradley (London: Penguin, 1999).

Laurel C. Schneider, "Isaiah 12," *Feasting on the Word, Year C*, vol. 4, ed. David L. Bartlett and Barbara Brown Taylor (Louisville KY: Westminster/John Knox, 2010).

Patricia Tull, "Isaiah 12," *Feasting on the Word, Year C*, vol. 4, ed. David L. Bartlett and Barbara Brown Taylor (Louisville KY: Westminster/John Knox, 2010).

OF THE FATHER'S LOVE
BEGOTTEN

Isaiah 12:2-6

Introduction

The first twelve chapters of Isaiah are filled with gloom and doom. In those chapters, the prophet presents a dark picture in which God is upset with the northern kingdom of Israel, the southern kingdom of Judah, and the ruling power of the day, Assyria. When we read Isaiah 1–12, we get the idea that the future looks bleak for just about everyone.

But tucked away in those dark chapters are a few rays of light. Those rays of light come from a series of short messianic prophecies that look to the future and promise coming peace and prosperity for the people of Israel.

In chapter 7, we read a verse that we looked at last week: "Therefore the Lord himself will give you a sign. Look, the young woman is with child and shall bear a son, and shall name him Immanuel" (Isa 7:14). Things were bleak, no doubt, but one day in the future Immanuel would come.

In chapter 9, the prophet envisions a day when "a child has been born for us, a son given to us; authority rests upon his shoulders; and he is named Wonderful Counselor, Mighty God, Everlasting Father, Prince of Peace. His authority shall grow continually, and there shall be endless peace for the throne of David and his kingdom" (Isa 9:6-7a).

In chapter 11, the prophet writes, "A shoot shall come out from the stump of Jesse, and a branch shall grow out of his roots. The spirit of the LORD shall rest on him, the spirit of wisdom and understanding, the spirit of counsel and might, the spirit of knowledge and the fear of the LORD. His delight shall be in the fear of the LORD" (Isa 11:1-3).

Our focal passage for this week, though not specifically a messianic prophecy, provides another ray of light within Isaiah 1–12. In Isaiah 12:2-6, the prophet looks to the day when God will gather the exiles and restore them to their land. At that time, the people will rejoice and say, "Surely God is my salvation; I will trust, and will not be afraid, for the Lord GOD is my strength and my might; he has become my salvation" (v. 2).

In the midst of all of this gloom and doom, the prophet Isaiah invited the people to look to the future, to a day when the glory of the Lord would be revealed in their midst. Although Isaiah 12:2-6 is not typically a Christmas text, it turns out to be an ideal Christmas study. When we look at these verses and overlay them on the Christmas story, we see four ways Jesus fulfilled Isaiah's promise.

Salvation

Isaiah predicted there would be a day when the people exclaimed, "Surely God is my salvation; I will trust, and will not be afraid, for the Lord GOD is my strength and my might; he has become my salvation" (12:2). That promise was best fulfilled when Jesus came into the world over 700 years later. Jesus came into the world as the long-awaited Messiah, the Savior, the one who came to bring salvation to the world.

But what exactly is this salvation Jesus came to bring the world? The Jews thought it involved political power and world dominion. Others have described salvation primarily in terms of going to heaven and avoiding hell. Others have pictured it in terms of personal peace and happiness. Still others have depicted salvation as the time when we turn from our sin to embrace a new way of life. Depending on whom you ask, salvation has a number of possible definitions.

Perhaps the best way to think of it is to consider the Latin word *salus* from which the word salvation comes. *Salus* means "health, wholeness, or well-being." To experience salvation, then, means we finally become spiritually healthy, whole, and well. When Jesus said in John 10:10, "I came that they may have life, and have it abundantly," he was giving us this concept of salvation. Salvation is abundant life, life as God intended people to live it.

The Apostle Paul gave us a vivid picture of that life in the Philippians 3 passage we studied a few weeks ago. He wrote about having his past made whole ("forgetting what lies behind" Phil 3:13), his future made whole ("straining forward toward what lies ahead" Phil 3:13), and his present made whole ("I press on toward the goal for the prize of the heavenly call of God in Christ Jesus" Phil 3:14). God had mended all three dimensions of his life—past, present, and future—and Paul was filled with joy, even in a Roman prison cell.

As we celebrate the birth of Jesus this year and every year, we celebrate the fact that he has brought us salvation and made us healthy. Our past is forgiven, our present is filled with purpose, and our future is filled with hope. In his birth, life, death, and resurrection, Jesus brought us salvation, so we finally can celebrate what Isaiah predicted the people of God would one day declare: "Surely God is my salvation; I will trust, and will not be afraid" (12:2).

Joy

The salvation Isaiah wrote about was connected to joy: "With joy you will draw water from the wells of salvation" (12:3). Certainly, once we find the wholeness and health we're supposed to have, the result is joy. Once we've experienced a forgiven past, a purposeful present, and a hopeful future, we can't believe how wonderful life is! Joy is the natural result of salvation.

When the angel announced the birth of Jesus to the shepherds it was a message filled with joy: "I am bringing you good news of great joy for all the people: to you is born this day in the city of David a Savior, who is the Messiah, the Lord" (Lk 2:10-11). Blow the horns, beat the drums, and sing at the top of your voice, for the one who will make salvation possible for every person has just been born!

Jesus' birth was filled with joy, his life was filled with joy, his resurrection was filled with joy, and our lives are supposed to be filled with joy, too. The most infallible proof of the presence of

God in our lives is our joy. They will know we are Christians by our love, for sure, but they will also know we are Christians by our joy.

Of all people, those of us who have drawn from "the wells of salvation" should be filled with joy. It is a joy that notices and treasures "the little things":

> As much in my fifties as in my forties, I feel much of the time like a child. I get excited about the kinds of things that excite a ten-year-old. The first snow of the year, for instance. The smell of breakfast. Buying things, especially books, which, like a child, it is less important for me to read than simply to have. Getting things in the mail. Going to the movies. Having somebody remember my name. Remembering somebody's name. Making a decent forehand in tennis. Being praised. Chocolate ice cream. And so on. (Frederick Buechner, *A Room Called Remember* [San Francisco: Harper & Row, 1984] 14)

Learn from him. There is joy. There is a life of wholeness and health.

Gratitude

There is a natural progression in Isaiah 12:2-6. First, Isaiah celebrates salvation. Then he mentions joy. And then he mentions gratitude. Once we've experienced salvation and joy, isn't gratitude the next logical step? "And you will say in that day: Give thanks to the LORD, call on his name; make known his deeds among the nations; proclaim that his name is exalted" (12:4).

In one of his sermons, Fred Craddock told the story of a woman who shared with him the moment of her conversion. She said it happened when, as a young mother, she went into her baby's bedroom to tuck the child into bed. Her baby was fast asleep, though, and the woman said she stood at the foot of the baby bed overcome with emotion. This child was amazing, miraculous, and a gift beyond all reckoning. That moment at the foot of the baby bed, the woman told Craddock, was her conversion experience.

"I knew I had to have Someone to thank," she said.

What one of us can't identify with that? Once we've experienced the salvation Christ came to give us, and once we've felt the joy he brings into our lives, we, too, know we have to have Someone to thank. And when we look around us and realize how blessed we are, how amazing, miraculous, and precious our life is, how can we do anything but join Isaiah in expressing gratitude?

And, like that woman's amazement at the gift of her child, we realize that our salvation and the joy it produces are sheer gifts, too. We love God because God first loved us. It all started with the fact that God is crazy about us, has redeemed us in Christ, and now invites us to join the party. We are to receive the gift of God's delight and then spend the rest of our lives in gratitude.

Singing

The final step in the progression is to break out in song: "Sing praises to the LORD, for he has done gloriously; let this be known in all the earth. Shout aloud and sing for joy, O royal Zion, for great in your midst is the Holy One of Israel" (12:5-6).

There is an old hymn titled "How Can I Keep from Singing?" Written by a Baptist minister named Robert Lowry, the hymn begins with this verse:

My life flows on in endless song, above earth's lamentations,
I hear the sweet, tho' far-off hymn, that hails a new creation.
Through all the tumult and the strife I hear the music ringing,
It finds an echo in my soul. How can I keep from singing?

In light of the salvation, joy, and gratitude we have because of Christ, how can we keep from singing? It is no coincidence that the Advent season is filled with music. Everywhere we go, we hear "Joy to the World," "O Come, All Ye Faithful," and "Silent Night." But for those of us who have been touched personally by the One born in Bethlehem, we not only hear those songs, we join in singing them.

Even if we can't carry a tune, we just have to sing this time of the year. Once we have experienced the abundant life Jesus came to bring us, how can we keep from singing?

Conclusion

As mentioned before, Isaiah 12 is not typically studied during Advent. We tend to look at those other passages in Isaiah, the ones promising a coming messiah. But when we think of Isaiah 12:2-6 in light of Jesus' birth, it makes that birth sparkle. What Isaiah was predicting in the eighth century BC was fulfilled completely when Jesus was born.

Isaiah saw a coming day of salvation—the very reason Jesus came into the world.

Isaiah saw a day of joy—and Christians have known for centuries that they should be the most joyful people alive because of who Jesus was and what Jesus did.

Isaiah saw a day of thanksgiving—and Christians are filled with gratitude for the incredible blessings they enjoy as a result of Jesus' birth.

Isaiah saw a day of singing—and Christians join together during Advent to sing at the top of their lungs as they celebrate what that baby means to them personally.

Isaiah 12:2-6, though not ordinarily associated with Christmas, turns out to be a perfect description of the progression many of us move through this time of the year. We realize afresh what Christ has done for us, we feel the joy stirring again within us, we are overcome with gratitude for our blessings, and we break out in song to express our feelings.

Notes

Notes

4

WITH THE ANGELS
LET US SING

Luke 2:8-20

Central Question

What makes this familiar story new, fresh, and worth sharing?

Scripture

Luke 2:8-20 8 In that region there were shepherds living in the fields, keeping watch over their flock by night. 9 Then an angel of the Lord stood before them, and the glory of the Lord shone around them, and they were terrified. 10 But the angel said to them, "Do not be afraid; for see—I am bringing you good news of great joy for all the people: 11 to you is born this day in the city of David a Savior, who is the Messiah, the Lord. 12 This will be a sign for you: you will find a child wrapped in bands of cloth and lying in a manger." 13 And suddenly there was with the angel a multitude of the heavenly host, praising God and saying, 14 "Glory to God in the highest heaven, and on earth peace among those whom he favors!" 15 When the angels had left them and gone into heaven, the shepherds said to one another, "Let us go now to Bethlehem and see this thing that has taken place, which the Lord has made known to us." 16 So they went with haste and found Mary and Joseph, and the child lying in the manger. 17 When they saw this, they made known what had been told them about this child; 18 and all who heard it were amazed at what the shepherds told them. 19 But Mary treasured all these words and pondered them in her heart. 20 The shepherds returned, glorifying and praising God for all they had heard and seen, as it had been told them.

Reflecting

"Silent Night" is known as the world's favorite carol. It is consistently voted number one in polls, ahead of the runners-up "Away in a Manger" and "O Come, All Ye Faithful." It is so popular it has its own webpage (www.silentnight.web.za).

Nearly all Christians know the carol, and many also know the legend of its origin. But things are not always as they appear. Yes, the text was written by Joseph Mohr and the music, for guitar, was written by Franz Gruber. The hymn was first sung at Midnight Mass on December 31, 1818, at St. Nicholas Church in Oberndorf, Austria. In this first performance of the song, "Silent Night" was sung by two male vocalists, accompanied by guitar, and joined by the choir on the final two lines of each verse. However, the lore of this story having been written in haste is not true. The legend of it being written on short notice for the guitar instead of the organ, because church mice had eaten through the bellows of the organ, is not accurate. Rather, Mohr wrote the poem in 1816. Two years later, Mohr asked Gruber to set the poem to music so that it could be sung at Midnight Mass. Menacing mice do not get any credit for this carol!

This carol might have been lost, like many other Austrian folk carols, had not the popular singing Strasser Family performed it in 1832 as a "newly discovered Tyrolean folk carol" (*The Penguin Book of Carols*, 301). As a result of one of their concerts, the carol was published, but without mention of either Mohr or Gruber. Only after recourse to the law were Mohr and Gruber able to prove their authorship.

> How might Christmas itself be a forgotten treasure in our culture? How can we retrieve and cherish the true meaning of the season?

The most popular of Christmas carols was nearly forgotten. When it was rediscovered, its authors nearly received no acknowledgement, much less credit, for their beautiful work. Although the legend of the menacing mice makes a charming story of the carol's origins, the true story better undergirds its value and enhances its power and meaning.

Studying

Luke's account of the birth of Jesus can be found in many images, tableaus, and picture books. These verses are read in churches of all sizes, retold in homes by families gathered at tables or around the tree, and dramatized in humble children's pageants as well as elaborate theatrical productions. We tell this story over and over again, sometimes weaving in additional details from Matthew's Gospel—or from folklore.

Luke 2:1-20 can be subdivided into three parts. Verses 1-5 introduce the setting for the birth of Jesus in Bethlehem. Verses 6-7 describe the actual birth. The final part, verses 8-20, tells of "the manifestation of the newborn child to the shepherds and the reaction of all who heard of it to the birth and manifestation" (Fitzmyer, 392). Angels make the birth announcement.

Commentators distinguish between three different types of reactions by the characters in Luke's Gospel. First, there is the reaction of the shepherds (vv. 15-17, 20). Then there are the reactions of those to whom the shepherds relate their story (v. 18). Finally, there is Mary's reaction (v.19).

The shepherds first received the angelic message. They hurry to verify the news they have heard. After they see the child lying in the manger, they respond with praise and glory to God for all that they have seen and heard. Their function for Luke is not that of eyewitnesses to verify the story, but rather as individuals who show "spontaneous trust in the heavenly message, which results in their hastening to the child.... [They are an] example of the kind of spontaneous faith of which the Lucan Gospel is full" (Fitzmyer, 397).

The second reaction is of the townsfolk who hear the shepherds' story. Their reaction is astonishment: they are "amazed" by the news the shepherds bring (v. 18). For some interpreters, this moment is "a clear parallel with the scene surrounding the

circumcision and naming of John the Baptist for there also all were astonished" (Brown, 428). Whether this observation is true or not, Mary's reaction is a noticeable difference between these two stories in Luke. According to Brown, "Only Mary is reported to have kept the events, interpreting them in her heart" (428).

Mary's is thus the third reaction Luke reports. The Gospel writer contrasts how Mary responds with the first two groups. The shepherds go forth telling all that they have seen and heard, and those who hear are "amazed." Mary, however, holds these events close in her heart, keeping them to herself. Mary is a believing woman, as Elizabeth indicates in verse 1:45, but she treasures and ponders the meaning of this child and the events surrounding his birth within herself. The people of Bethlehem heard the news, but it didn't lead them to investigate further. Brown links this distinction with the parable of the sower in Luke 8. Perhaps, claims Brown, the others are much like "the audience described in the parable (v. 8:13), 'they hear the word, receive it with joy, but have no root.' Whereas Mary is one of 'those who, hearing the word, hold it fast in an honest and good heart' (8:15)" (428).

Why is the announcement of Christ's birth made to shepherds? The shepherds were most likely Jewish. In classical Greek, Latin, and Old Testament literature the word shepherd "was often used for a political and sometimes for a military leader" (Fitzmyer, 395). In this setting, however, no such connotation is intended. These are shepherds in the literal sense. Shepherds have a long-standing biblical connection with Bethlehem, which is the town of David, the shepherd who tended the flocks of his father, Jesse.

> How can the carol "Silent Night" help us to follow Mary's example and "treasure" and "ponder" the significance of Christ's birth?

Fitzmyer adds one final aspect regarding shepherds. We are not to take them as examples of sinners who receive the word of salvation brought by heavenly messengers. Neither are they to be seen as "examples of the poor, since the implication of 'their flock' may mean that they owned them" (Fitzmyer, 396). Instead, Fitzmyer suggests "their presence is another example in the infancy narrative of Luke's predilection for the lowly of human society" (Fitzmyer, 396). Brown adds that the shepherds can also be viewed as forerunners of the future believers "who will glorify God for what they have heard and will praise God for what they have seen" (Brown, 429).

Understanding

Luke's ageless and powerful story holds many deep and significant truths. Shepherds, the lowly and outcasts of society, were entrusted with a story that promises to upend the world as it was known. A drama unfolded that only a few saw at its beginning. Only a few truly understood its meaning, even as Jesus entered adulthood.

In the usual nativity scenes, the shepherds linger at the manger with their sheep, watching the holy family. In Luke, however, they do not linger. Rather, the shepherds "come in haste, and then leave to go spread the news" (Vinson, 62). Even though the shepherds seem unlikely choices to be the first recipients of the good news, much less the first evangelists, "they take to their job with enthusiasm" (Vinson, 62).

We should take cues from the shepherds. Hear the good news that is proclaimed this season and receive it. Take action: go, seek after, and find what has been revealed. Share with others the wonder of this new life which has come.

But do not forget Mary and her reaction. Mary held these events close to her heart and reflected on all that they mean. Therefore, continue to reflect on the meaning of Christmas, well past the unwrapped gifts, dinner celebrations, and special services of worship. Remain within the unfolding drama of the coming of Christ in this season, allowing the presence of God's gift to deepen the meaning of your life and experiences.

What About Me?

• *Keep the story of Christmas fresh.* We tend to skim the story of Jesus' birth because we are so familiar with it. How can we keep from getting bored by a story that has been told to us, read by us, and preached among us for so many years? How can we reclaim the sense of awe?

• *Look around you for the person who might be hearing this story for the first time.* Might this be the preschooler in your church? The international student from a country that is closed to the gospel? Whomever it is, how can you share this story with someone who has never heard it before? Imagine yourself into the shoes of such a person as you read this story. Listen for the fear—and later, the joy—of the shepherds. Consider the brightness of the night sky. What might Joseph and Mary been thinking as shepherds came so soon after Jesus' birth?

• *What not-so-accurate images of this story need reconsideration?* Maybe you sang a song as a young child about the innkeeper who said "no room, no room" when Joseph came knocking for a place to stay. Commentaries reflect that this is neither a fair nor accurate treatment of the innkeeper. Still it can be a hard image to erase.

• *Let December 25th become the beginning, not the end, of your Christmas discoveries.* Follow the tradition of the ancient church in celebrating the twelve days of Christmas, *beginning* on December 25th, as a season of reflection on the meaning of Christ's birth. Follow the example of Mary in treasuring these meanings and discoveries in your heart. Let this Christmas season become a renewal of life within you and around you. Allow yourself to grow alongside this child born in a manger, Christ the Savior.

Resources

Raymond E. Brown, *The Birth of the Messiah: A Commentary on the Infancy Narratives in the Gospels of Matthew and Luke*, rev. ed. (New York: Doubleday, 1993).

Bill Egan, "Silent Night: The Song Heard 'Round the World," <http://www.silentnight.web.za/history/index.htm>.

Joseph A. Fitzmyer, *The Gospel According to Luke I–IX*, The Anchor Bible (New York: Doubleday, 1981).

The Penguin Book of Carols, ed. Ian Bradley (London: Penguin, 1999).

Richard B. Vinson, *Luke*, Smyth & Helwys Bible Commentary (Macon GA: Smyth & Helwys, 2008).

WITH THE ANGELS LET US SING

Luke 2:8-20

Introduction

We Christians have a tendency to turn poetry into prose. We take a biblical passage that is mysterious, intriguing, and wonderful and flatten it out. We make it understandable and boring. We remove all of the mystery, intrigue, and wonder from it and transform it into a three-point devotional or a Power Point presentation.

That is especially true, I think, at Christmas. If we're not careful, we can remove all of the poetry from the Christmas story. We can take the incredible scene in Luke 2 of angels singing, shepherds worshiping, and Mary treasuring these things in her heart and make it into a drab picture filled with trite "lessons for life." Once we have "explained" the first Christmas, all of the magic is gone from it.

I've been wrestling with that this week as I've tried to write about Luke's all-too-familiar version of the Christmas story. I don't want to turn poetry into prose, but I do want us to grapple again with the meaning of Jesus' birth. Let's prayerfully tiptoe to the text, filled with wonder and awe, and think about the implications of the birth of this baby.

In particular, let's approach this story about the angels singing and try to sing along with them. When we think about these verses, there are several reasons we can join the angels in song.

Confidence in a Fearful World

The angel told the terrified shepherds not to be afraid. In so doing, the angel sets the stage for Jesus, who will utter those same words over and over again in the Gospels. To people feeling terrified and overwhelmed, Jesus consistently echoed the angel, saying, "Don't be afraid."

To the ruler of the synagogue, who had received the shocking news of his daughter's death, Jesus said, ""Do not fear, only believe" (Mk 5:36).

To Simon Peter, who was both amazed and terrified at the number of fish he had just caught, Jesus said, "Do not be afraid; from now on you will be catching people" (Lk 5:10).

To Peter, James, and John, who were shocked by the vision they saw on the Mount of Transfiguration, Jesus said, "Get up and do not be afraid" (Mt 17:7).

To his followers, after telling them to seek first the kingdom of God, Jesus said, "Do not be afraid, little flock, for it is your Father's good pleasure to give you the kingdom" (Lk 12:32).

To the stunned women who caught the first glimpse of him after his resurrection, Jesus said, "Do not be afraid" (Mt 28:10).

To the disciples, who had to come to grips with his impending crucifixion, Jesus said, "Do not let your hearts be troubled" (Jn 14:1).

Jesus went from person to person telling them not to be afraid and to have confidence in God's sovereignty. The angel's "Do not be afraid" was merely one of many in the Gospels.

Jesus' followers believed him and started saying it themselves. In his second letter to Timothy, Paul wrote, "God did not give us a spirit of cowardice, but rather a spirit of power and of love and of self-discipline" (2 Tim 1:7). In his celebration of the unconditional love of God, Paul reminds the Roman Christians that they "did not receive a spirit of slavery to fall back into fear" (Rom 8:15).

John picks up the baton, too, and writes: "There is no fear in love, but perfect love casts out fear; for fear has to do with punishment, and whoever fears has not reached perfection in love" (1 Jn 4:18).

All those New Testament admonitions to flee fear and trust God are music to our ears because fear is such a pervasive part of our culture—and our own lives. Fear seems to be in the very air we breathe.

I once read an article that listed various phobias that are now part of our society. On the list was arachabutyrophobia: the fear of getting peanut butter stuck on the roof of your mouth! Suffice it say, it was a long list. It reminded me that there is no shortage of fear in our world. While we might have escaped the trauma of arachabutyrophobia, most of us would have to admit that we experience more than our share of fear, too.

Jesus finished his Sermon on the Mount (Mt 5–7) by telling the story of the house on the sand and the house on the rock. Both houses had to face the storm with the same wind, the same rain, and the same danger. But one house had been built on a foundation of sand, and one house had been built on a foundation of rock. The house on the sand fell, and great was its fall. The house on the rock stood firm, unscathed by the storm.

That story comes at the end of the profound sermon Jesus had just preached about how to build a life. If we follow his way, live by his truths, and build on his directions, he says, we will be able to withstand whatever storms life hurls at us. We don't have to worry or fret. Our life-house is sturdy, anchored to the One born in Bethlehem, crucified at Calvary, and risen to live in your heart and mine. We are safe and secure, and we do not have to be afraid.

We can have confidence in a fearful world.

Good News in a Bad-News World

The angel announced to the astonished shepherds, "I am bringing you good news of great joy for all the people" (Lk 2:10). We can join the angels in song once we realize how good our good news really is.

Bad news abounds in our society. I begin each day with a cup of coffee (okay, several cups of coffee) and the newspaper. I start with the sports page and read it word by word. Then I move on to the front page, where I simply scan the headlines. I can't bear to read the front section's stories in depth because I get too depressed. That front section is loaded with news about murders, robberies, child abuse, economic woes, and other disasters. To read those articles word by word would plummet me into the pit of despair. It's hard to believe that much bad news happens every day.

That's why we so desperately need the "good news of great joy for all the people." In a bad-news world, we have the good news of the gospel, which stands sovereign over all of those articles in the newspaper. Jesus Christ has been born in a stable, lived a God-focused life, died on a cross, rose from the dead, and lives within every person who will acknowledge his lordship. Reading this story, as we do every Advent, is the perfect antidote to the bad news we hear every day.

This is an ideal time of year to remember that the Bible is brimming with good news. As Karl Olsson wrote in his book *Come to the Party* (Waco TX: Word Books, 1972),

> It abounds in party clothes, perfumes, and ointment; in music, dancing, and frolic. Jesus came and wherever he went there was a party, "the feast of the bridegroom" (see Lk 7:31-34). Or there was a party and Jesus was there. It would be tedious to list all the allusions to feasting, but the parables of Jesus are full of it, and it is significant that the last gathering of the disciples was a celebration. (16-17)

Somehow, those of us who have received this good news about feasting and celebration have managed to turn it into something burdensome, boring, and religious. The greatest need in the church today is to rediscover the good news all over again, to be astonished again at the wonder of the gospel. We have good news in a bad-news world, and we dare not forget it or take it for granted.

Salvation in a Searching World

The angel then said to the shepherds, "To you is born this day in the city of David a Savior, who is the Messiah, the Lord" (Lk 2:11). This baby born in Bethlehem was the long-awaited Messiah, the one who would rescue his people from their distress.

The Jews had been looking for this Messiah for centuries, but they envisioned him as an earthly king who would restore them to a place of peace and prominence. Jesus came as a spiritual king, not interested in ruling in the halls of government, but in ruling in the hearts of individual people.

When we read those horrible headlines in the daily paper, or when we look at the mess we've made of our own lives, we sense something is wrong. Why this alienation, emptiness, and dissatisfaction? Who or what can fix what is wrong with us and with our world?

Maybe heredity is to blame. Maybe it's the environment in which we live. Maybe it's the education system. Maybe it's the political system of our society. Maybe it's something else altogether. But whatever it is, we know something is wrong with us and the people around us. The "system" is broken.

The Bible's answer is that we're all afflicted with a condition called "sin." We all have a bent toward selfishness, ego, and personal gain. So, according to the Bible, we need more than a sociologist, psychologist, or politician. We need a savior. We need someone who can forgive us, show us a new way to approach life, and instill hope within us as we embark on this new journey.

The New Testament writers tell us that Jesus came into the world to do precisely those three things. He came to be our savior.

In his life, he gave us a new pattern for living.

In his death, he forgave our sins and made us right with God.

In his resurrection, he gave us hope that even death cannot defeat us.

Even people who do not consider themselves "religious" seek these things. We all want a new way of approaching life, a way of joy and purpose. We all want to know that our sins are forgiven and that we don't have to be shackled to our past mistakes. And we all want to have hope, to believe that death is not the final curtain but that something or Someone lies beyond the curtain. Whether we know it or not, we all hunger for salvation.

At Christmas, the world gazes at a baby in a manger. Though the world may not understand all of the implications of the baby's birth, the New Testament writers did. This one is the Savior, the Messiah, the Lord, they said.

Follow him, and you can find salvation in a searching world.

Conclusion

Many of us grew up playing hide-and-seek. Whomever was "it" would count to ten and then yell, "Ready or not, here I come!" Then he or she would seek out all of those who were hiding.

At first, it was fun to be hidden. We felt smug and secure if we had a good hiding spot, one where we couldn't be found. But if we stayed hidden too long, it stopped being fun. After a while, we would cough, move around, or do something else to attract attention. After all, no one wants to be lost forever. Eventually, we all want to be found.

When Jesus had his famous encounter with Zacchaeus, he was dealing with a man who was finally coming out of hiding. Zacchaeus had been hiding behind his wealth, perhaps, or his prestige, or his reputation, or who knows what else. But he came out of hiding, met Jesus, and had his life changed. Jesus's comment about the encounter was, "The Son of Man came to seek out and to save the lost" (Lk 19:10).

Jesus came to seek out those who are hiding. He wants to give us confidence in a fearful world, good news in a bad-news world, and salvation in a searching world.

Isn't it time to come out of hiding?

Notes

Notes

5

Bearing Gifts
We Traverse Afar

Matthew 2:1-12

Central Question

What gifts do I have to bring to Jesus?

Scripture

Matthew 2:1-12 2 In the time of King Herod, after Jesus was born in Bethlehem of Judea, wise men from the East came to Jerusalem, 2 asking, "Where is the child who has been born king of the Jews? For we observed his star at its rising, and have come to pay him homage." 3 When King Herod heard this, he was frightened, and all Jerusalem with him; 4 and calling together all the chief priests and scribes of the people, he inquired of them where the Messiah was to be born. 5 They told him, "In Bethlehem of Judea; for so it has been written by the prophet: 6 'And you, Bethlehem, in the land of Judah, are by no means least among the rulers of Judah; for from you shall come a ruler who is to shepherd my people Israel.'" 7 Then Herod secretly called for the wise men and learned from them the exact time when the star had appeared. 8 Then he sent them to Bethlehem, saying, "Go and search diligently for the child; and when you have found him, bring me word so that I may also go and pay him homage." 9 When they had heard the king, they set out; and there, ahead of them, went the star that they had seen at its rising, until it stopped over the place where the child was. 10 When they saw that the star had stopped, they were overwhelmed with joy. 11 On entering the house, they saw the child with Mary his mother; and they knelt down and paid him homage. Then, opening their treasure chests, they offered him gifts of gold, frank-incense, and myrrh. 12 And having been warned in a dream not to return to Herod, they left for their own country by another road.

Reflecting

Three kings, traveling far across the landscape from the East, have been strongly etched in our images of the Nativity. Though the Gospel of Matthew does not confirm the number of these visitors, scenes rarely ever depict a different number. Nor, it should be said, does Matthew confirm their royal status. He merely says they are "magi," wise men. The idea that they were in fact kings came later.

Certainly, the carol "We Three Kings" has contributed to how we dramatize and visually represent the Christmas story. "We Three Kings" is an American carol from the nineteenth century. Though "it is almost certainly based more on fiction than fact," it remains a favorite for use in Nativity plays, Christmas dramas, and men's trios (*The Penguin Book of Carols*, 377). John Henry Hopkins, an Episcopalian minister, wrote both the words and tune. It was written to be sung by a trio of men, each having a solo in the second, third, and fourth verses and singing in parts on the first and fifth. The refrain was written for a full chorus to sing in four-part harmony.

The three "kings" were first given names in the *Armenian Infancy Gospel*, dating from the sixth century. They were called Melkon, king of the Persians, Gaspar, king of the Hindus, and Balthasar, king of the Arabs, and the story became well established in Europe by the eighth century. Gaspar, also known as Caspar, brought gold, symbolizing the royalty of the infant Jesus. Melchior, originally Melkon, offered frankin-cense, an incense used in temple worship, emphasizing Jesus' divinity. Finally, Balthasar came with myrrh, a spice that was mainly used for embalming, and thus

> Do you think the Wise Men understood the possible symbolic associations of their gifts? Is it possible that our actions have significance beyond what we intend or can imagine?

has clear associations with Jesus' death (*The Penguin Book of Carols*, 377).

Subsequent traditions about the magi, including the familiar carol, have expanded upon our remembrance of these exotic figures beyond what is narrated in Matthew's Gospel. Yet the embellishments are consistent in bestowing reverence and honor upon the child who is born and in confessing the Christ child's significance for humankind through the valuable offerings the Wise Men give.

Studying

Which has had the greater influence on how we understand these ancient visitors from the East: Matthew's Gospel or later traditions? Consider for a moment that Matthew gives no indication of the number of these visitors—only that there were more than one. Furthermore, he nowhere indicates that they were "kings."

The English word "magi" comes to us in a roundabout way. In Latin, the word *magus* (plural, *magi*) means "mage" or "magician." (You can see the family resemblance between *magus* and "magic.") In ancient times this word referred to "one who is wise in reading the stars and the signs of the time" (Witherington, 55). But even this is not the ultimate origin of the word. The Greeks borrowed the word from the Persian *maga*, meaning "great one," and referring to a particular sort of "wise man" or soothsayer. The magi of

According to Herodotus (ca. 450 B.C.E.) magi (the plural of *magus*) were a priestly caste among the sixth-century Medes who specialized in interpreting the significance of human affairs through the observation of celestial phenomena (7.37) and the interpretation of dreams (1.107–108, 120, 128; 7.19). When the Persians conquered the Medes (ca. 550 B.C.E.), the magi apparently adopted the Zoroastrian religion of their conquerors, transforming it to the extent that they became its priests. Cicero (*On Divination* 1.91) indicates that no one was able to assume the throne of Persia without mastering the scientific discipline of the magi. In subsequent centuries the term came to be loosely applied all across the Mediterranean world to those adept in various forms of secret lore and magic. Thus by the first century C.E. it was applied to those of a particular class rather than to those of a particular culture or citizenship. (Gloer, 539)

ancient Persia were astrologers and sages who sought to read coming events in the stars.

It seems logical to us that there would be three such visitors because of the three distinct gifts they bring. Obviously, this is mere conjecture, which may or may not be accurate.

More important than their number or occupation is the relevance behind the appearance of these exotic travelers in the Christmas story. One important role they play is to serve as "representatives of the Gentile world that recognize who Jesus is and properly worship him" (Witherington, 57). At the end of Matthew's Gospel, Jesus tells the disciples to go into all the world; here at the beginning, the world comes to Jesus to worship him.

The magi come asking where they might find the one who has been born king of the Jews. Herod would know immediately that they were not inquiring about him, because he was not *born* king of the Jews. Rather, he "bought" his kingship through his friendship and alliance with the Romans. The magi also announce they have come to worship this king. In the Near Eastern world, it was widely believed that kings were in some way divine, perhaps the son of a god, as in ancient Egypt. Their stated intention to perform acts of worship suggest that they may have had such a mindset (Witherington, 61).

The magi arrived at Herod's palace because they observed the newborn King's star (Mt 2:2). But the astronomical evidence was not enough to confirm their discovery. They went to Herod's palace seeking additional information they could not acquire through astronomy. They needed guidance from the writings of the Old Testament prophets (Witherington, 63). Therefore, they sought out Herod and the religious teachers at his court.

Understandably, Herod becomes disturbed—as does all of Jerusalem with him. The appearance of the magi and the prophecy they inquired about indicated that political change was on the horizon. Such change was rarely smooth in the region, and all of Jerusalem would certainly have anticipated some kind of unpleasant upheaval. New leadership would not be welcome to the current elite, "who were indebted to and partially dependent on the current regime for their own power and wealth" (Witherington, 64). Contrast this response to that of the magi, who, upon finding the place where the child was residing, experienced great joy.

The gifts from their "treasure chests" were gold, frankincense, and myrrh (v. 11). Frankincense and myrrh are expensive gifts. The incense is a resin drawn from the incense tree (genus *Boswellia*) that grows in Arabia. A high grade of frankincense was costly, bringing upwards of six denarii per pound, "which is equivalent to six days of wages for a day laborer, salary for one week" (Witherington, 67). Myrrh comes from myrrh trees, grown in Arabia and Ethiopia. Myrrh was also costly, going for as much as fifty denarii per pound. These imported items "were used as spices, for cosmetic purposes, for magical practices, at ceremonial occasions, and even as medicine" (Witherington, 67). While these gifts might reflect the wealth of the magi, Witherington points out that "they certainly are intended to reflect the worth of the Christ child" (67).

Scholars generally agree that the Gospel of Matthew was intended primarily for a community of Jewish believers in Jesus. The Gospel writer often interprets the story of Jesus' birth in light of the life of Moses. Of particular note is the presence of an evil king who orders the slaughter of innocent children in the birth stories of both Moses and Jesus. Witherington cautions us not to read too much of Moses into this story, however. For example,

> Jesus is not born in Egypt, he does not serve in Pharaoh's court, he does not flee from Egypt, the angel of death comes after Egyptian not Jewish children unlike Herod, and the magi are not portrayed at all in a negative light here, unlike the counselors of Pharaoh. (56–57)

Instead, Witherington draws our attention to the similarities in the birth of Solomon. Believing this is one key to understanding this story, Witherington claims that "Matthew is remembering the story of Solomon, who was visited by the Queen of Sheba who bore gifts from Arabia" (58). This makes the strong connection that Jesus is a son of David—just like

Solomon—bringing to fulfillment the promise that restoration and salvation will come through the line of David.

Understanding

The magi have many lessons to teach us. As noted above, they serve Matthew's purposes by representing the Gentile world that recognizes the identity and significance of Jesus. It was important for Matthew's predominantly Jewish community of believers to grapple with the theme of Gentile inclusion. In this story, people outside of Judaism not only take notice of the Messiah's birth, but follow the sign, seek additional information, and bring him gifts.

The magi are depicted as people outside the faith community, yet even so, it is they who recognize that a new King of the Jews has been born. Perhaps these stargazers see what "insiders" miss, because they are accustomed to looking for signs and pondering their meanings.

The magi returned to the land from which they came—albeit by a different route. Perhaps we are to do likewise. Upon making our journey of preparation and celebration during Advent and Christmas, we are to return to our homes, our jobs, and our activities, but by a different route. Just as the magi surely were not able to return unchanged, we certainly should not return to our lives as if they will be the same as we left them after Thanksgiving. The world is different now. We have seen and heard from God like never before. Will we remember this as we return to our ordinary activities and schedules?

An additional perspective on this passage engages the senses to answer some questions. There is another thread running through this text. As Witherington explains, this story "revolves around answering three 'where' questions" (57). First, where was Jesus born? Second, after hearing of the threat of Herod, where did the child go? And last, following the death of Herod, where did this child travel?

Where does Jesus reside now that Christmas Day has come and gone?

What About Me?

• *Now that we have made our journey through Advent and Christmas, what gifts can we bring to Jesus?* The gifts the magi brought were of great value. What valuable items might you offer to show what it means to you that God has given us Jesus? Don't think merely in terms of dollar amounts. How can you worship Christ by giving of your time or your talent? What other intangible valuables— control, status, reputation, etc.—can you offer to Jesus as a sacrifice?

• *With whom do we identify in this story?* When have we been "foreigners" or "outsiders" to the things of God? When have we been "insiders," too wrapped up in the life of the institution to notice the new things God is doing in our midst? When have we been led to fall before Christ and offer him our gifts? When have we done violence to Christ or his cause in order to preserve our own positions of power?

• *Where is the Christ child in your life?* Consider answering the "where" questions in the "Understanding" section with respect to your own life and experience. Where in your life have you experienced the birth of Christmas? Where has the spirit of Christmas gone now that Christmas Day has passed? Now that Advent and Christmas have passed, where is Jesus in your life?

Resources

W. Hulitt Gloer, "Magi," *Mercer Dictionary of the Bible*, ed. Watson E. Mills et al. (Macon GA: Mercer University Press, 1990).

The Penguin Book of Carols, ed. Ian Bradley (London: Penguin, 1999).

Ben Witherington III, *Matthew*, Smyth & Helwys Bible Commentary (Macon GA: Smyth & Helwys, 2006).

BEARING GIFTS
WE TRAVERSE AFAR

Matthew 2:1-12

Introduction

Some passages in the Bible immediately connect with our lives. When we read the Sermon on the Mount, for example, we know that it has practical and profound implications for the way we live. When we read of Zacchaeus's encounter with Jesus, we can easily identify with the empty frustration Zacchaeus must have felt and his desperate attempt to do something about it. And when we read Paul's words of joy from a prison cell, we get instant encouragement. Some biblical passages are easily accessible.

But, to tell the truth, some are not. Some biblical passages seem strange to us, and we wonder if they have anything to say to modern people. The story of the Wise Men coming from the East to visit the Messiah is one of those, at least for me. It's hard for me to connect to that story and apply it to my own experience.

I'm not a wise man from the East. I've never seen a mysterious star in the sky guiding me anywhere. And I've never been on a long journey seeking the long-awaited Messiah. You and the people you will teach this Sunday are probably in the same boat.

At first glance, it seems that the story of the three Wise Men is a nice piece of ancient folklore that is intriguing, enchanting... and irrelevant. It doesn't seem to intersect with our own experience.

But as I read the story again this week, it hit me that the basic outline of the Magi's encounter with Christ is actually the basic outline for anyone who has an encounter with Christ. As we follow the movement of this story, we see that it may not be as strange and inaccessible as we first thought.

Caught by a Vision

There has been much speculation and interest in the star that guided the Wise Men. Books by the dozens have been written about this mysterious star and the mysterious Magi who followed it. Whatever that strange star was, it caught the attention of the Magi, and they decided it would take them to the promised Messiah.

Our own journey to the Messiah begins not by chasing a star but by catching a vision of who Jesus is and how rich our life can be if we follow him. For me, that journey started as a young boy when, through church and the example of my parents, I saw the difference Christ could make in someone's life and wanted to experience that difference for myself. Others have caught a vision of who Jesus is and the difference he makes by reading books, listening to music, hearing sermons, or observing the lives of friends or coworkers. However it happens, we start our journey toward Jesus because we are captivated by him and his offer of abundant life.

We stay on the journey because we continue to have this vision of a life lived in partnership with Christ. We envision teaching our class with his kind of scholarship, raising our child with his kind of love, conducting our work with his kind of diligence, or being part of a church that does his kind of ministry.

The Magi were motivated by a star; we are motivated by a vision—and where there is no such vision, the people wither and die. But where there is this vision of Christ and of life in union with him, people thrive and experience purpose and joy.

Relentlessly Pursuing Jesus

This was not an easy journey the Wise Men took. No one knows where they started their journey, but they might have come from Persia, a distance of about 800 miles. On foot, that trip would have taken several months. The Magi had to have a lot of grit and determination to keep at it.

Even today, a journey of 800 miles is no easy task. But we tend to lose sight of how difficult it was to travel that far in the first century. The Magi had no air-conditioned cars or jumbo jets as they searched for the Messiah, but they had plenty of robbers, heat, wind, rain, and weariness.

So let's give these Wise Men their due. They were determined to find Jesus, and they persevered until they did. For them, looking for the Messiah was the search of all searches, and they were not going to be denied.

Their relentless pursuit of Jesus serves as a reminder that those of us on the Jesus Way still have to be relentless in our pursuit of him. We don't have to deal with the same problems the Wise Men had to deal with, but we have plenty of our own.

We have to persevere in the face of doubt. Though we would prefer to walk by sight, we've been given the difficult assignment of walking by faith. That means we don't have all of the answers. It means we occasionally stumble into doubt and have to keep on trusting God anyway. It means there might be times when we don't know God and cling to the hope that God still knows us.

We have to persevere in the face of personal problems. The follower of Jesus is never exempt from difficulties, and we have to hang in there with God through sickness, sorrow, confusion, conflict, and a wide assortment of other problems.

We have to persevere in the face of mystifying evil. The headlines tell us of murder, child abuse, accidents, and other horrifying things, but, with faith the size of a mustard seed, we keep on trusting in a good and loving God.

We have to persevere in the face of a secular culture that sees us as pious fools. Walking the Jesus Way puts us on a narrow road, and many in our society will not understand us at all. We live as sojourners and foreigners in a strange land, and the temptation is great to quit being "so religious" and to be like everyone else.

Suffice it to say, modern pilgrims had better have the same tenacity as the Magi. Eugene Peterson entitled one of his books *A Long Obedience in the Same Direction* (20th anniversary ed., Downers Grove IL: InterVarsity, 2000). That's a good description for the journey of the Wise Men, and it's a good description for the journey of any modern person who is following Jesus.

Offering Their Gifts

Matthew never says there were specifically three wise men; he simply reports that three gifts were offered: gold, frankincense, and myrrh. Those three gifts accurately foreshadowed the kind of messiah Jesus would be. Gold represented royalty, and Jesus would become the King of Kings. Frankincense was used in worship, and Jesus would become the great High Priest. And myrrh was used in embalming, and Jesus would become the sacrificial Lamb who took away the sins of the world.

There could have been three wise men, or there could have been twenty. Whatever their number, they came bearing gifts. And eventually we do, too. After catching a vision of Christ and pursuing him relentlessly, we offer him our own gifts. By that, I mean we offer him our financial gifts. There is probably no more pragmatic verse in the Bible than this one in the Sermon on the Mount: "For where your treasure is, there your heart will be also" (Mt 6:21). If we truly love Jesus, our checkbook will prove it. Follow the trail of our check stubs, and we will inevitably discover our heart.

But offering our gifts is more than that. We also offer him our personal gifts of talents, interests, and abilities and trust that these things can be used to help construct the kingdom of God. In truth, the talents, interests, and abilities of ordinary people like us are the building blocks of the kingdom. God takes my interest in writing, your knack for numbers, someone else's ability to cook, and someone else's talent for singing and uses them all to build a kingdom of love.

If we think of the world as a cosmic tug-of-war between good and evil, love and hate, our assignment is to take hold of the rope and pull for good and tug for love. By using our own gifts and investing them in God's kingdom, we're doing our part to cooperate with God in this cosmic struggle that is being played out before our very eyes.

Every day we take who we are and what we can do and grab hold of the rope. Every day we offer our meager gifts to the King and do our part to be instruments of good and agents of love.

Going Home by a Different Way

At the end of this passage, Matthew says, "And having been warned in a dream not to return to Herod, they left for their own country by another road" (Mt 2:12). The Magi adjusted their itinerary to avoid King Herod's sinister plot. They were meant to be pawns in Herod's scheme to locate the baby so he could be killed, but they decided not to cooperate. They returned to their country by another road.

No one who meets Christ returns home the same way he or she came: "If anyone is in Christ, there is a new creation: everything old has passed away; see, everything has become new!" (2 Cor 5:17). Our encounter with Christ affects the way we think, how we treat our families, how we do our job, how we spend our money, and how we set our priorities. Once we come to Christ, all things become new.

Toward the end of the Sermon on the Mount, Jesus talks about two roads—a wide, heavily traveled road that leads to destruction, and a narrow, sparsely traveled road that leads to eternal life. Long before Robert Frost wrote about the road less traveled, Jesus encouraged people to get on that second road. When we become a follower of Jesus, we step off of one road so we can travel on another.

The Magi literally followed a different road home, but I would like to think they followed a different spiritual road home, too. They got off of the Herod road—the road of jealousy, anger, and power—and got on the Jesus road—the road of peace, joy, and love. They decided not to cooperate with King Herod and cast their lot with baby Jesus.

It is fair to say, I think, that any encounter with Jesus that doesn't put us on a different road is not a real encounter.

Conclusion

This passage gives us all we know about the Wise Men. Matthew is the only New Testament writer to mention them, and he never mentions them again. Even after reading Matthew 2, we're left scratching our heads and pondering puzzling questions: What was this mysterious star? Who were these unnamed Magi? Where did they come from? How many were there? What finally became of them? Immortalized in the song "We Three Kings," the Magi are a part of every Christmas season, but they remain enigmatic and elusive.

But if we step back and look at Matthew's account of these men, and if we use a little imagination, we can readily identify with them. For all of their strangeness, their journey to find Jesus becomes our journey to find Jesus.

Like them, we receive a vision and decide to embark on a journey to discover Christ.

Like them, we have to be relentless in our pursuit of Christ and not get discouraged.

Like them, we offer Christ our best gifts, our own version of gold, frankincense, and myrrh.

And like them, we're radically changed by our encounter with Christ and find ourselves on a completely new road home.

With just a touch of imagination, the "inaccessible" episode of the three Wise Men can be transformed into a story very much like our own.

O God, as we stand at the beginning of a New Year, make us wise men and women. Make us wise so that we will search for Christ in the right places and in the right ways. And show us clearly the road we should take in the year ahead. In the name and spirit of Christ we pray, Amen.

Notes

Notes

nextsunday
STUDIES

1 Peter
Keep Hope Alive

This study of First Peter focuses on keeping hope alive in the face of pressures and circumstances that could possibly extinguish it completely, or worse, turn authentic faith into a pale replica of the real thing.

Advent Virtues

The phrase "holiday rush" is not an exaggeration. The frantic pace required to purchase gifts, bake holiday foods, and attend Christmas parties, plays, and performances takes its toll; we arrive at Christmas Day exhausted. Within the context of December busyness, the ancient Christian season of Advent takes on new meaning and acquires renewed importance. May God instill the virtues of *hope*, *peace*, *joy*, *love*, and *faith* in each of us this Advent.

Apocalyptic Literature

This study examines five apocalyptic texts in the Bible—from Zechariah, Daniel, Matthew, and Revelation. With each new year bringing a new prediction of impending doom, it is always a perfect time to get the story straight. Apocalyptic literature does not address the future. It addresses our present.

Approaching a Missional Mindset

The World isn't the same as it once was. We must be the church in a new place, in unimagined ways, and with a wider range of people. Engage your small group with the radical and refreshing challenge of developing a "missional lifestyle."

Baptist Freedom
Celebrating Our Baptist Heritage

What makes a Baptist a Baptist? Of course, the ultimate answer is simple: membership in a local Baptist church. But there are all kinds of Baptist churches! What are the spiritual and theological marks of a Baptist? What is the shape and the feel of Baptist Christianity?

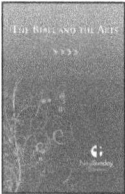

The Bible and the Arts

God has used artistic expression throughout the centuries to convey truth, offer blessing, and urge believers to deeper faithfulness. In modern life, artistic expression flourishes, from movies to books to music to paintings to photographs. Sometimes artists are intentional about trying to portray God's truths. Other times, perhaps God is working even when the artist is unaware of it. As believers, we may hear and see God at work in many art forms.

The Birthday of a King

The first four lessons in this unit draw inspiration from a traditional interpretation of the Advent candles as the Prophets' Candle, the Bethlehem Candle, the Shepherds' Candle, and the Angels' Candle. The final lesson, which occurs after Advent, celebrates the theological meaning of Jesus' birth as described in the prologue to John's Gospel.

Challenges of the Christian Life

The way of the cross is difficult, and taking Jesus seriously means looking honestly at how we fall short of God's best hopes for us and seeing how much we need God's grace. For all of us there are times when we need to remember that Christ is our saving grace and recommit ourselves to the journey of faith, rediscovering, again and again, the life-giving purpose described in the book of Ephesians.

Christ Is Born!

Even in the midst of difficult circumstances, Advent is a time when we can find hope. Much like today, people in the 1st century church faced struggles. Examining the Gospel of Matthew, lessons include "Waiting for Christ," "Preparing for Christ," "Expecting Christ," "Announcing Christ," and "The Arrival of Christ."

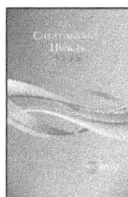

Christians and Hunger

These sessions challenge us to apply gospel lenses and holy imagination to what literally gives us energy to live: food. With God's grace, we have the opportunity to imagine communities where tables are large and all are fed.

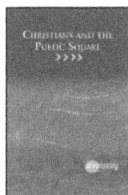

Christians and the Public Square

Politics and faith are tricky areas for Christians to negotiate. The First Amendment to the Constitution guarantees religious freedom for all Americans. As Christians who are also citizens, questions abound: How do we distinguish between faithful and unfaithful forms of civic engagement? How do we give Caesar his due while giving our all to God?

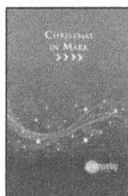

Christmas in Mark

In the early chapters of Mark, we will encounter a Christmas story. This story, however, will not be quite like the one told by other Gospel writers, but it will resonate with the reality of your life. Mark doesn't deny the beauty or reality of the nativity; however, he seems to believe that Christmas begins—the gospel begins—when Christ intrudes upon the hard realities of life.

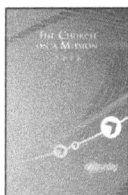

The Church on a Mission

What does it mean to be a church on a mission? The lesson of Acts 1:8 is that we must simultaneously carry out Christ's mandate at home, in our region, in places that have been our blind spots, and around the world.

Colossians
Living the Faith Faithfully

Paul's letter to the Colossians begins with a high-minded philosophical defense of the faith, but concludes with a collection of extremely practical advice for living by faith. This study addresses the questions many Christians face today, helping them apply Paul's practical advice in their own lives.

Easter Confessions

Easter confession is often found on many different lips in the Gospel of John. When we listen carefully, those ancient confessions still echo into this new millennium.

Embracing the Word of God

We live during a time of transition in Christian history. Basic assumptions about the truth of the Christian faith are being questioned, not only by nonbelievers, but by Christians themselves. First John offers a starting point for understanding of what it means to "be" Christian.

Esther: A Woman of Discretion and Valor

The book of Esther is not a record of historical facts as such. Rather, it is a magnificent narrative that refuses to interpret life as being driven by coincidence or happenstance. In the otherwise unknown characters of Esther, Haman, and Mordecai, we trace the movement of the divine hand as God collaborates with God's risk-taking people to rescue them from the hand of their enemies.

Facing Life's Challenges

This study explores four significant challenges common to most persons of faith: the challenge of new light, the challenge of time's limit, the challenge of living with mystery, and the challenge of authentic spirituality. Although these issues are neither simple nor easy to ponder, this study effectively leads us in confronting these challenges.

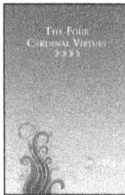

The Four Cardinal Virtures

Christians are learning how to distinguish between members of a church and disciples of Christ. Discipleship involves developing virtues in those who come to our churches seeking life, salvation, grace, mercy. If we want to have something to offer a world in desperate need, then we must return to virtues like discernment, justice, courage, and moderation. We must return to the hard and glorious work of making disciples.

Galatians
Freedom in Christ

Paul wrote with fiery passion, as you will notice from the opening paragraphs of this letter to the Galatians. But his language reveals that he was writing about a crucially important issue—the very nature of salvation in Christ.

A Holy and Surprising Birth

Christmas begins here—discover these five love stories from the book of Luke and renew your appreciation of God's laborious effort to birth our salvation.

How Does the Church Decide?

An array of decisions draw energy and time from church members. These decisions may be theological, such as mode of baptism, aesthetic, such as the color of the sanctuary carpet, or functional, such as the selection of a new minister. This study will consider how the church has made its decisions in the past to help guide our decisions today.

Is God Calling?

Witness the varying forms of God's call, the variety of people called, and the variety of responses. Perhaps God's call to you will become clearer.

James
Gaining True Wisdom

If we'll be honest with God and ourselves as we study what James says, we can make great strides toward wisdom and a living faith.

Life Lessons from Bathsheba

Who was Bathsheba? She was a complex figure who developed from the silent object of David's lust into a powerful, vocal, and influential queen mother.

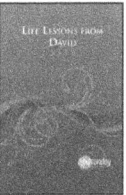

Life Lessons from David

In the Bible, we catch David in the various stages of the human journey: childhood, adolescence, adulthood, and senior adulthood. From the biblical treatment of the stages of David's life, we can land some insights to assist us in better understanding the human journey.

The Matriarchs

The matriarchs of Genesis offer their lives as a testimony of faith, perseverance, and audacity. We learn from their mistakes and suffering. We will gain the hope of Hagar, the joy of Sarah, and the audacity of Rebekah as we are challenged to examine our prejudices and our insecurities while studying Esau and Jacob's wives.

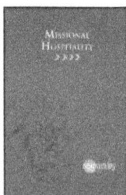

Missional Hospitality

If we are serious about following Jesus, we will be people of open hearts, open hands, and open homes. In other words, as followers of Jesus we will practice the fine art of hospitality. In lesson one, we reflect on hospitality to strangers. In lesson two, we address hospitality to the poor. In lesson three, we focus on hospitality to sinners. In lesson four, we learn about hospitality to newcomers. Lesson five reminds us about our hospitality to Christ.

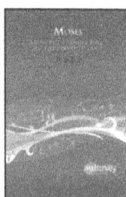

Moses
From the Burning Bush to the Promised Land

We would do well to trace the life of Moses so we might discover how his life changed, both personally and as Israel's leader, as he learned what it meant to love God with all his heart, soul, and strength.

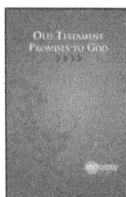

Old Testament Promises to God

Some individuals may feel that our promises couldn't possibly mean anything to God. Perhaps the real question is this: under what circumstances should or do we make such promises? The Old Testament contains several examples of people making promises to God, using the unique form of a biblical "vow."

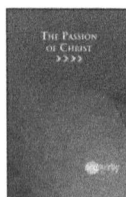

The Passion of Christ

The four lessons in this unit highlight the faith struggles of the early disciples. In lesson one, Jesus addresses the issues of faith and practice. In lesson two, we meet Judas who, like us, struggled with God's Kingdom and human kingdoms. In lesson three, the issue of temptation reminds us that our faith journey is a constant challenge. Lesson Four invites us to remember Peter's experience of "faith failure." Peter's failure, however, is not the final word. There is forgiveness.

The Prayer Life of Jesus

The study of Jesus' prayer life can deepen our own prayer practices. These five sessions examine the importance of prayer at various stages of Jesus' life and ministry. He made no important decisions without consulting God.

Proverbs for Living

Long ago, a collection of wise teachers committed themselves to the ways of God and collected this wisdom into what we know as the book of Proverbs. These four lessons explore the simple truth of Proverbs: there is a good life to be had—a life lived in faithfulness to God.

Qualities of Our Missional God

Too often we are tempted to let "numbers" drive missions. The book of Numbers reminds us that missions is motivated by something deeper. Missions reflects the heart and nature of God. If we can just get past the math, we can see God's nature clearly in the book of Numbers. . . in the wilderness.

The Seven Deadly Sins

What exactly is sin? Just as we organize our cupboards and our schedules to make sense of our lives, Christian thinkers have organized sin into a number of categories in order to understand and surrender these patterns to God. The notion of "seven deadly sins" emerged as a way to recognize specific dangers to our spiritual lives. The purpose of the book is to guide people away from sin and into a wise and godly life.

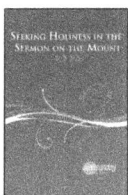

Seeking Holiness in the Sermon on the Mount

The Sermon on the Mount has long been recognized as the pinnacle of Jesus' teaching. But with this importance in mind, it's easy to think of Jesus' teachings as lofty and idealistic, offering little guidance for everyday life. Perhaps Jesus' sermon allows us to see beyond ourselves, beyond our own failures and shortcomings— revealing God's intention for our lives.

Spiritual Disciplines
Obligation or Opportunity?

The spiritual disciplines help deepen a believer's faith and increases his or her intimacy with Christ. In this study, we take a deeper look at some of the disciplines and consider their practice as a response to God's love.

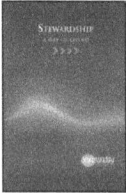

Stewardship
A Way of Living

Great News! Stewardship is not about money! At least not *just* about money. Certainly, stewardship relates to money, and, yes, we need to tithe. However, stewardship branches out into multiple areas of life. Properly practiced, this act of service can lead to peace and purpose in living.

The Ten Commandments

When the Ten Commandments are in the news, it is usually because a judge or teacher has hung them up on the walls. The Ten Commandments do not need to be posted or even preached nearly so much as they need to be practiced and viewed as life-giving, joyful affirmations of a better way of life.

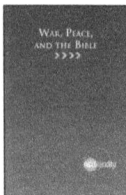

War, Peace, and the Bible

As people of faith, we are faced daily with an expectation that we participate in violent actions, our willingness to allow violence in the world to continue, and our response to violence in our lives. Is there a place for war and violence in our faith?

What Would Jesus Say?
A Lenten Study

To address what Jesus would say, we need to discover what Jesus did say. These lessons will attempt to help us understand Jesus' teachings and apply them today.

NextSunday Studies are available from   NextSunday Resources

www.ingramcontent.com/pod-product-compliance
Lightning Source LLC
Chambersburg PA
CBHW070548030426
42337CB00016B/2398